SELF-DEFENSE YOU CAN
LEARN AT HOME!

Ten lessons of basic, practical self-defense now arranged for home study. Bruce Tegner has combined the best techniques from many fighting styles into a method of street defense which is more useful and more effective than any of the specialties—judo throws, aikido holds or karate blows. This is not karate for contest; it is not judo for sport; it is not ceremonial jiu jitsu; it is not make-believe movie stunt fighting—it is effective, practical self-defense for today. It is self-defense you can learn and remember.

The ten step-by-step, fully-illustrated lessons cover a complete course of basic self-defense, with sensible advice, reasonable explanations and easy-to-follow instruction.

BOOKS BY BRUCE TEGNER

BRUCE TEGNER'S COMPLETE BOOK OF KARATE

BRUCE TEGNER'S COMPLETE BOOK OF AIKIDO

BRUCE TEGNER'S COMPLETE BOOK OF JUKADO SELF-DEFENSE
    Jiu Jitsu Modernized

BRUCE TEGNER'S COMPLETE BOOK OF JUDO

KARATE: Self-Defense & Traditional Sport Forms

KARATE & JUDO EXERCISES

STICK FIGHTING: SPORT FORMS

STICK FIGHTING: SELF-DEFENSE

DEFENSE TACTICS FOR LAW ENFORCEMENT:
    Weaponless Defense & Control

SELF-DEFENSE NERVE CENTERS & PRESSURE POINTS

BRUCE TEGNER METHOD OF SELF-DEFENSE:
    The Best of Judo, Jiu Jitsu, Karate, Yawara, etc.

SELF-DEFENSE FOR BOYS & MEN:
    A Physical Education Course

SELF-DEFENSE YOU CAN TEACH YOUR BOY:
    A Confidence-Building Course, Elementary School Age

SELF-DEFENSE FOR WOMEN: (With Alice McGrath)
    A Simple Method for Home Study

SELF-DEFENSE FOR GIRLS & WOMEN: (With Alice McGrath)
    A Physical Education Course

BLACK BELT JUDO, KARATE, JUKADO

JUDO & KARATE BELT DEGREES: Requirements, Rules

AIKIDO and Jiu Jitsu Holds & Locks

JUDO FOR FUN: Sport Techniques

SAVATE: French Foot & Fist Fighting

KUNG FU & TAI CHI: Chinese Karate & Classical Exercise

Additional titles in preparation

BRUCE TEGNER

METHOD OF

SELF-DEFENSE:

10 LESSONS FOR HOME STUDY

SECOND REVISED EDITION

THOR PUBLISHING COMPANY

VENTURA   CALIFORNIA

Tegner, Bruce.
    Bruce Tegner method of self-defense: the best of judo,
jiu jitsu, karate, savate, yawara, aikido, and ate-waza.
Completely rev. ₍Ventura, Calif., Thor Pub. Co., 1971

    127 p. illus. 22 cm. 1.95

    1. Self-defense.   ɪ. Title.

GV1111.T4 1969   796.8′1   74-153398
SBN 87407–003–1   MARC

Library of Congress   69 ₍3₎

← ———————————————————————— →

ACKNOWLEDGMENTS: RICHARD WINDISHAR
assists the author in demonstrating techniques
throughout the book. Neil Ziegler assists in photos
251-268.

BRUCE TEGNER METHOD OF SELF-DEFENSE: *The Best of Judo, Jiu
Jitsu, Karate, Savate, Yawara, Aikido, Ate-Waza*

SECOND REVISED EDITION

*The first version of this book was published in 1960. A completely
revised edition was published in 1969 with all new photos and all
new text. This edition is revised from the 1969 edition; the material
on pp. 121-125 is new in this edition.*

> *First edition: November 1960*
> *Second printing: October 1962*
> *Third printing: December 1964*
> *Fourth printing: February 1967*
> *Completely revised: October 1969*
> *Second revised edition: May 1971*

Manuscript prepared under the supervision of
ALICE McGRATH

Published simultaneously in the U.S. and Canada

———————————————————————————

THOR PUBLISHING COMPANY
P.O. Box 1782
Ventura, California 93001

PRINTED IN THE UNITED STATES OF AMERICA

Review excerpts of other BRUCE TEGNER books:

BRUCE TEGNER'S COMPLETE BOOK OF JUKADO SELF-DEFENSE: Jiu Jitsu Modernized

"This is the most useful book on the Oriental fighting arts that I have ever seen."
Michael H. Dygert, LIBRARY JOURNAL

SELF-DEFENSE YOU CAN TEACH YOUR BOY: A Confidence-Building Course (for elementary school age boys)

"The easy to learn defenses are safe and practical."
JOURNAL OF HEALTH, PHYSICAL EDUCATION and RECREATION

SELF-DEFENSE FOR GIRLS (with Alice McGrath, a physical education course for girls and women in secondary schools.)

". . . The authors' advice is sound and their methods could easily be practiced in gym classes."
Charles Curran, LIBRARY JOURNAL

SELF-DEFENSE NERVE CENTERS & PRESSURE POINTS

"Students and teachers of unarmed fighting will find much valuable source material in this attractive book."
SCHOLASTIC COACH

SELF-DEFENSE FOR BOYS & MEN (A physical education course for secondary schools.)

". . . recommended for school libraries. The text deserves inspection by physical education instructors."
Charles Curran, LIBRARY JOURNAL

KUNG FU & TAI CHI: Chinese Karate Forms and Classical Exercise

". . . recommended for physical fitness collections."
Charles Curran, LIBRARY JOURNAL

CONTENTS

PREFACE TO THE REVISED EDITION

The original version of this book was published in 1960. At that time, the new, modern ideas which Bruce Tegner expressed were received with a mixture of shock and enthusiastic approval. Since then, so many people have accepted Bruce Tegner's ideas (including many who were previously outraged by them) that it is hard to realize the stunning impact of the Tegner concepts in 1960. Now, he has been paid the compliment of frequent imitation; now the entire subject field shows evidence of the strong influence of his thinking and his methods.

Among the ideas which Bruce Tegner put forward is the notion that change and adaptation are necessary if the material is to remain vital, modern and relevant. In this he opposed the traditionalists who insist on a rigid and ceremonial approach to teaching and use of the unarmed arts. Using a rational method of evaluating and presenting weaponless fighting skills, Mr. Tegner has become the most successful popularizer of what were formerly cult practices and he has been the most consistent critic of out-dated, dangerous, socially irresponsible methods of teaching and practice.

Mr. Tegner has developed many ideas which are in direct contradiction to traditional attitudes. His ideas and his methods are the result of a life-long, full-time involvement in this work. A brief résumé of his career will indicate the background and accomplishments which make him the most experienced and authoritative teacher in this subject field.

Both his parents were professional teachers of judo and jiu jitsu. From the age of two, Bruce Tegner was instructed in many specialties of weaponless and stick and sword fighting by Oriental and European experts. By the time he was twelve years old, he was a teaching assistant at his parents' school and by the time he was sixteen years old he was a full-fledged teacher.

At the age of fifteen, he had achieved the junior black belt in judo contest and in formal work. At the age of seventeen, he won his second degree black belt in judo and was then the youngest second degree black belt holder on record in the United States.

In 1949, he was the California State judo champion, winning the championship in open competition in Santa Barbara. At the time that he won this championship he was teaching unarmed combat in the U.S. armed forces and was coaching army sport judo teams. In 1952, when he completed his service, he opened his own school in Hollywood which he operated until 1967.

In his long career of teaching, Mr. Tegner has instructed thousands of people in class and private lessons. His students have been men, women and children and they have come from every walk of life.

He has taught students of varying abilities with markedly different needs and goals. He has taught the disabled. He has trained law enforcement officers to a high degree of practical skill and he has taught basic, simple self-defense. He has trained tournament players to competition excellence and he has taught judo and karate as physical fitness pastimes. He has originated movie and TV fight scenes and prepared the actors to perform them.

From all this rich and varied experience, Mr. Tegner has been able to test old concepts, experiment with new ideas and devise original solutions to special problems.

Among the modern ideas which Mr. Tegner has introduced to the teaching of practical self-defense are these:

> Sport use and self-defense use of fighting skills are different. The goals of tournament training are vastly different from the goals of basic self-defense. Individuals learning practical self-defense need not engage in contest nor practice contest-oriented procedures.

> A combination of the most effective techniques from many fighting styles is more useful, as basic street defense, than is any single one of the specialties—judo throws, or aikido holds, or karate blows.

> Basic self-defense should consist of techniques which are effective for individuals with a moderate level of skill; this eliminates the necessity for training to reach the championship level of skill needed for contest. Instead of learning hundreds of specific defenses against hundreds of specific attacks, basic self-defense should consist of a relatively small group of actions which can be

used flexibly against many types of attacks. A small group of defense actions can be *remembered* for emergency use without life-long practice; a moderate level of skill can be *maintained* by most individuals without life-long practice.

Another original idea which Bruce Tegner introduced is the concept that many of the techniques of judo, jiu jitsu, aikido and karate are impractical for most people; only the exceptionally skilled individual in top physical condition could use the high kicks, the intricate locks, the complicated throws, and the spectacular leaps taught in the traditional styles of weaponless fighting. The traditional method of teaching self-defense, in practice, eliminates from the instruction those people who would benefit from it to the greatest degree.

A black belt, which indicates expert proficiency in the performance of weaponless fighting skills, does not prepare an individual to be a good teacher. Bruce Tegner introduced the concept that basic self-defense can be taught effectively by people who have had teacher training, but no previous experience in the specialty of weaponless fighting. This concept has been proven correct by the great success of physical education teachers who are teaching self-defense units in secondary schools throughout the country. A high level of performance skill is not a requirement for good teaching; a physical education teacher has more important qualifications for teaching body skills than does a black belt holder.

At this writing, Mr. Tegner has 25 books in print in this subject field—with additional titles in preparation. In the years during which he has been writing (and revising) these books, he has learned a great deal from the students who study exclusively through books. From the thousands of letters which have come to him from these people, Mr. Tegner has been able to evaluate the needs and problems of the men, women and children who consider him their teacher—for they have no other access to instruction. In response to these needs and problems, this book has been completely revised and shaped to give you the best possible home-study guide for learning basic self-defense.

PRE-INSTRUCTION

SAFETY IN PRACTICE

The major guarantee of safety is a *concern* for safety. This may sound obvious, but it is a new approach to the teaching of self-defense. The traditional manner of teaching self-defense assumes that it does not matter if the students got hurt while learning the techniques. The old-fashioned teacher of self-defense does not differentiate between teaching a modern course of useful self-defense and training a samurai warrior.

You need not hurt your partner to learn, nor need you endure unnecessary pain.

TAPPING FOR SAFETY

Tapping is a way of saying "stop" to your partner. Get into the habit of tapping from the very first day of practice. Tapping is better than a verbal signal. Tapping eliminates the need to say "ouch" and it can be used when a vocal signal would be difficult (as in the practice of a choke).

1 2

Tapping the floor or your partner, or yourself, are the three ways of stopping the action.

1. Tap your partner to signal "stop."
2. Tap the floor to signal "stop."

You tap for "stop" when the technique has been applied correctly and just as you begin to feel pain.

You tap for "stop" if you feel that the technique is being applied incorrectly. You will be told more about this in the text in the comments on correcting mistakes.

You and your partner must be conscientious about using the tapping signal and responding to it. You must stop the *instant* you are given the tapping signal. It is risky and foolish to play games with this instruction. Trying to see how much pain you can take before tapping for release will not help you learn and it will increase the possibility of injury.

Do not work with a partner who refuses to tap for release or who does not immediately respond to your tapping signal.

SLOW MOTION FOR SAFETY

Work slowly, in the beginning. Rushing through the techniques before you know them well is not a good way to learn and it may result in rough and unnecessarily painful practice. As you develop skill, you will develop control. When you have greater control, you can increase the speed of your application of techniques. A smooth, correct manner of working is a better way of learning than fast, sloppy execution of the technique.
OBEY THE SAFETY RULES.

KICKING FOR SELF-DEFENSE

Is kicking dirty fighting? Is the person who defends himself against street attack a poor sport if he kicks? The curious attitude toward kicking as dirty fighting results from confusing sport activity with street assault. A street attack is not a sporting event and the attacker does not follow any rules of sportsmanship; why should the *victim* be required to follow rules which prevent an effective response to the attack?

If you are fighting by rules which *both* opponents have agreed to observe, then it would be very poor sportsmanship to break the rules. In the old-fashioned fight for "honor" the combatants agreed to the fight and then agreed upon the conditions of the fight. In a street attack, the victim is an unwilling participant; the assailant is ordinarily bigger and stronger. It doesn't make any sense to limit the victim to defense techniques which give the advantage to his attacker!

KICKING GIVES YOU AN ADVANTAGE

Your leg is longer and stronger than your arm. You can, therefore, deliver a more powerful blow with your foot and you can do it without coming within arm's reach of your adversary. This gives you considerable advantage. If you can stop the first action of an intended attack without getting hit, you may have finished the fight.

Using a kick for self-defense gives you the advantage of surprise. Street fighters are used to kicking (usually when they have their victim on the ground) but they are not used to a defense which includes kicking.

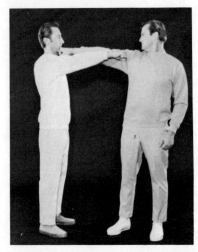

3

3. If your adversary is larger than you, his reach is longer. To move in close enough to punch him, you are in danger of getting punched first. You would have to be very fast to outpunch a street fighter in your first action.

4

4. If you try to use a judo throw as a first action, your adversary can punch you before you could grasp him. Only a highly skilled judo person could hope to use a judo throw to stop the intended attack.

5   6

5. Trying to grip the punching arm or wrist of a street fighter is a risky business for anybody except an experienced, skillful jiu jitsu- or aikido-trained individual. If you miss with this attempt, your adversary can complete his first action—which could end your defense.

6. If you use a kick you can stop the intended first action without coming into punching or grabbing range of the assailant. It is not always possible nor appropriate to use the kick as a first action, but where it is, it is effective, valid and practical.

IS KICKING BRUTAL?

Brutality cannot be defined in terms of techniques alone. A kick into the shin is less brutal than a powerful punch to the head. A throw which results in flinging the adversary to the ground could have more disastrous results than a kick into the knee; either technique could disable an assailant, but the kick would be less likely to cause permanent, serious injury.

Effective, modern self-defense is that which uses techniques appropriate to the situation. Self-defense is for protection, not for revenge or punishment. You are entitled to defend yourself; if you carry on the actions beyond the point necessary for your protection, your moral position is no better than that of your assailant. Kicking for self-defense is morally defensible when kicks are the effective, appropriate techniques for the particular situation.

T-POSITION

The T-position is similar to the fencer's stance. It is a position of good balance and it permits easy and quick shifting of body weight and foot position.

The name derives from the foot placement; if you place one foot back, as shown, and the forward foot at a right angle to it, your feet form a rough T.

The T-position is the one you should use for defensive balance too, to avoid getting pushed down or knocked off balance if you are struck.

7. The basic T-stance is as shown. Your lead foot should be the same as your lead hand. Most people will perform better if they lead with strong hand and foot. You should practice left and right lead T-stances and learn to use the defenses from your weak as well as your strong side.

Your feet are about shoulder width apart. Your knees are very slightly bent. The center of body mass is, ideally, between your feet. Your head is up, body erect.

From this position you can easily shift your weight to the rear foot for kicking, without loss of balance. You present less body target to your adversary. You are least vulnerable to being pushed off balance.

7

FALLS AND FALLING SAFETY

You need not learn judo falls to learn self-defense. Learning to fall correctly for practice of judo throws requires a great deal of practice and takes more time than a full course of basic self-defense.

If you follow the instructions carefully, you and your partner can practice the takedowns and trips in this course in a way which eliminates the need for falling skill. If you and your partner have been trained in judo falls, you may, of course, use them.

8. Avoid the mistake of breaking your fall by putting your hand down as shown; wrist and shoulder injury could result.

9. Avoid the mistake of falling onto your elbow.

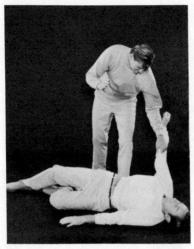

10   11

10.   Avoid the mistake of letting your head touch the ground.

The correct way of easing yourself down is to sit as close to the ground as you can and then roll gently back without allowing your wrist, elbow or head to absorb impact. This requires a bit of practice, but it is the safest way to fall without going into long training in formal judo falling techniques.

11.   As a practice procedure, sit down slowly, and roll back gently onto the floor keeping your arm fully extended (to avoid hitting wrist or elbow) with your head tucked forward somewhat to keep it off the ground.

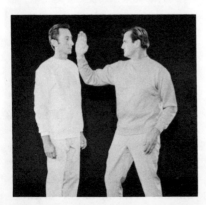

12

HITTING THE TARGET

Safe practice of the hand and foot blows can be done without making contact. You need not hit your partner to learn how and where to strike correctly. You can practice the essential action of the hand or foot blow and you can aim *at* the body target, but you do not have to hit it.

12. If you come within a few inches of the intended body target, that is close enough as a practice procedure. What you are learning is the correct way of doing the actions; you are not trying to prove that they are effective.

YELLING AS A DEFENSE AID

A sudden, loud, unexpected yell is startling and disconcerting. It can be used with your other actions to increase the effectiveness of your defense.

The usual reaction to a sudden noise is fear and disorientation. All the symptoms of fright—faster heart beat, trembling hands, accelerated breathing—can be induced by yelling at your opponent. Even if the disorientation period is very short, it will help you in your defense.

Yelling is an outward show of courage which has a psychological effect on your adversary. Whether or not you feel an inner courage, if you behave in a brave and determined manner, your assailant will perceive you as brave. Bullies do not look for brave adversaries; they want passive victims.

The act of yelling gives impact and a surge of extra power to your physical actions. Like the grunt which automatically accompanies lifting or pushing a heavy object, the yell tightens your abdomen and helps concentrate energy for most efficient self-defense.

If your practice location permits its, include yelling with the defense actions. It is not always possible to do this without being a nuisance to other people; if you can't actually yell, rehearse yelling in mental practice.

HOW TO FOLLOW INSTRUCTIONS

Before you begin to practice the physical techniques, read through all the pre-instruction material carefully. Give special attention to the safety procedures! Glance through the instruction; look at all the photos briefly.

Become acquainted with the gesture and style of the work you will be learning.

When you are familiar with the general material, you are ready to begin practice of the techniques. As you begin each lesson, re-read that lesson very carefully. Study the photos as you practice each separate technique or series of action.

After you have practiced the lesson, again re-read it and study the photos to refresh your concept of the actions and to help you retain them.

CORRECTING MISTAKES

Partners will find that they can more easily see the other person's mistakes than they can their own. This should be put to positive use. You should encourage each other to correct mistakes and you should both learn to accept correction as a help, rather than as a put-down.

A basic course of self-defense is not intended to make an expert of you, but should give you functional material which you can use for the rest of your life. Corrections should be made with this in mind. Perfection of technique is not what you are after; you want to correct each other to insure effective application of the defense actions. That is enough correction for basic self-defense.

HOW LONG SHOULD IT TAKE TO LEARN?

Individuals vary greatly in their ability to learn. Slow learning is not necessarily poor learning. Slow learners may retain their instruction as well as fast learners— sometimes even better. Don't rush through the course.

Individuals also vary greatly in their ability to learn types of techniques. What is very easy for one student might prove more difficult for another. You must go at your own pace. Work through each lesson until you feel that you understand it and can execute the techniques moderately well. The lessons are organized in a logical sequence, but they are not of equal length. Some individuals will find that they can learn a complete lesson in one session, while others might require several practice sessions to feel comfortably adept at the material in that same lesson.

FOLLOW THE ORDER

The lessons in this course were designed to be followed in order, from Lesson #1 through Lesson #10. You will make best progress if you do them in that manner. In each lesson after the first one, it will be assumed that you have studied and understand what has gone before.

If you come across a term or a technique which you do not understand or do not remember, look it up in the index at the end of the book, find it in the text and review it.

YOUR PARTICIPATION

My method of teaching you self-defense is similar to the modern method of teaching a language. From the first lessons, you will learn how to use the techniques in defense situations, just as you learn to say simple sentences when you have memorized a few words in a foreign language. Instead of making you practice techniques over and over without knowing how to use them, you will be encouraged to think of applications of techniques and different combinations of them.

As you progress in the course, you will build upon this simple "vocabulary" of defense actions and learn to put them together in more and more sophisticated ways.

WORKING WITH A PARTNER OR PARTNERS

You can become familiar with self-defense and even learn minimum techniques by reading the book and going through the defenses and techniques by yourself, but obviously that is not the best way to practice.

The ideal partner is someone who has the same degree of interest that you have and who will work through the course with you on an equal basis.

You could work with a passive partner, someone who simply allows you to practice on him, but that is not as much fun and it is not as useful as working with an active, interested partner.

If you have a group of three, you can take turns practicing in rotation, with the third person given the assignment of reading the instruction and watching for mistakes. If you have a group of four, change partners from lesson to lesson.

THE ATTITUDE OF CONFIDENCE

What pleases me the most about my students (those who have had personal instruction and those who have used my books) is that they rarely get into fights after learning self-defense. Because they feel that they can defend themselves, if necessary, they can run away from or decline a fight without losing their self-respect.

When faced with the possibility of assault or the challenge to fight, you have three possible choices: You can run away (situation permitting). You can submit to a beating. You can defend with spirit. Brave or cowardly behavior does not depend upon the choice you make; it depends on how you *feel* about the choice you make.

The most difficult and courageous behavior might be to submit to a beating. A true pacifist feels that it is less dignified to fight back than it is to submit. He does not feel demeaned because he does not fight and so he does not feel that he is behaving in a cowardly manner. I respect that point of view as valid and worthy, but it is not the choice I would make, nor is it likely that you would either, or you would not be reading this book.

Our choices, then, are whether to escape or fight in self-defense. Because I assume that any reasonable person would prefer not to fight, I also assume that it is rational to run away from a street assault without any loss of self-esteem.

The use of physical techniques of self-defense, then, should be limited to those situations in which you cannot escape, cannot get help, cannot talk your way out of trouble, or in any other way avoid fighting. To use the physical actions effectively, you must assume a show of spirit and confidence—even if you are frightened! Courage is not the absence of fear; courage is the ability to respond effectively in spite of feeling fear.

It is normal to feel frightened if you are confronted by the threat of violence. In spite of your fear you can put on the appearance of confidence and that will help you. If, instead of behaving like a helpless victim, cringing and cowering, you behave like an adversary, defending with spirit, it will undermine the confidence of the assailant. If you carry on your defense in a vigorous manner, as though you really mean to win, it will help you defend yourself.

In addition to yelling, mentioned earlier, your facial expression and body gesture can be important aids to self-defense. It will be useful to you to practice the techniques using forceful and vigorous gestures, even though you are not going to make contact on your partner.

DEFENSES DON'T WORK AGAINST FRIENDS

The defenses you will practice in this course have been selected for practicality and effectiveness. Testing them on friends is not valid. You can learn them with a friend, but you cannot prove them against a friend.

To prove the effectiveness of a technique you would have to apply it realistically. Obviously you cannot do that with techniques which result in considerable pain. For instance, you cannot doubt that a forceful kick into the shin causes a great deal of pain. In practice with your friend, you merely simulate the action and acknowledge the fact that it would work for street defense.

The element of surprise works for you in self-defense. Even in a friendly game you do not alert your opponent to your plays. In self-defense you would not tell your adversary what you plan to do. In demonstrating, or trying to demonstrate to friends, the effectiveness of techniques, you lose the advantage of surprise and you cannot make full-power contact blows. Self-defense is not a game. It is meant for and works in emergency situations—when you need it!

LESSON ONE

Before you begin to practice the techniques, read the pre-instruction. Be sure you understand the tapping signal; follow safety rules. Work slowly throughout this lesson.

OPEN-HAND BLOWS

The open-hand blow using the edge of your hand is the single most useful and effective hand blow you can learn. This is the blow which used to be called the judo chop or jiu jitsu chop and which is now called the karate chop. It is also called the sword-hand, the knife-blade, the hand-knife, the thousand-hand blow and many other fancy names. All these different names are used to describe the same hand blow. In this course we will refer to it as the open-hand slash, or as a slashing hand blow, or simply as a slash.

SLASH

There are a number of advantages to striking with the edge of your open hand. You can strike without hurting your own hand. You can hit in many different directions with equal effectiveness. You do not have to come in as close to deliver this blow as you would to hit with your fist. Most men can develop equal slashing proficiency with right and left hands. If you keep your hands open, you are prepared to defend yourself without a showing of hostility. Making a fist is a signal of readiness to fight; if you keep your hands open, you are ready to fight if you have to but your appearance is not hostile.

13. The correct way of hitting is shown. Your hand is very slightly cupped; thumb is held against the index finger; your hand is firm but not rigid.

Strike with the fleshy, muscle edge of your hand, slightly toward your palm. If you strike correctly using this blow, you can hit hard without injuring your hand. If you strike incorrectly, it hurts.

It is not necessary to callous or condition your hand for self-defense use of the slashing hand blow. Hand conditioning has no modern practical purpose and it can be permanently injurious to your hands.

If you give careful attention to correcting any mistakes you make in practicing the open-hand slash, you can hit as hard as is necessary for self-defense. Partners should take turns practicing the gesture of this blow as shown in the photo. You can strike onto the open palm of your partner without inflicting pain. Use a choppy action.

14.   Slash forward, as though to hit onto the nose.

15.   Holding your forearm horizontal, slash outward with a whipping action.

16.   Slash downward, using a choppy action.

14

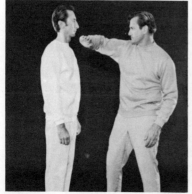

15   16

Avoid the mistake of extending your thumb away from
your hand; your thumb should rest against the index
finger. Avoid the mistake of hitting onto your little finger
or your wrist. If you tilt your hand forward, you will hurt
your finger bones, if you tilt your hand back, you will
hurt your wrist bones.

Practice striking lightly onto a table top to determine
whether or not you are hitting correctly. If you are slashing correctly, you will feel no pain at all when you hit
the hard surface lightly. Increase the force of the blow a
little at a time. Do not hit a full power blow unless you
are certain you are doing it correctly.

As you increase the force of your blow on the table, you
will feel a tingling sensation, but you should not feel
pain in your finger or wrist bones. If you do, alter the
position of your hand until you can slash properly. Because of individual differences in bone structure, each
person has a *slightly* different hand position for striking
a forceful blow without pain. You will find your own
personal correct position by following the procedure de-
scribed above.

For most uses of the open-hand slash, a choppy blow
with snappy recoil is best. The action is similar to that of
driving a nail, not that of pounding with a sledge.

17

HEEL-OF-PALM BLOW

17.   This blow has limited use, but is easy and effective.
Bend your wrist back, curl your fingers and strike upward
with the heel of your palm, as though hitting up under
your partner's chin. Make a sharp thrusting movement,
not a pushing action. Do not make contact.

BASIC KICKS

The stamp kick and the side-snap kick are the two most
effective, versatile, practical kicks you can learn for self-
defense. In sport karate, variations of these kicks are
used in spectacular ways against high body targets. Use
of the kicks in contest fashion requires long training and·

STAMP KICK

The stamp kick is made with the bottom of your shoe, the best striking area is directly in the middle of the foot.

18. Turn your side to your partner; this offers less target to an adversary. Be sure you are well out of his fist range. Draw your knee up and then stamp out toward his leg. Do not make contact.

In this lesson do not come as close to your partner as is shown in the photo. Practice the correct action of the kick and do not be concerned, at this point, with speed. You should practice to maintain balance, avoid stiff-legged kicking and keep your distance from your opponent.

In mental practice of the stamp kick, take a step back out of arm's reach of your adversary before you deliver the kick. Practice the kick alternately with your right and your left foot. Try to develop equal proficiency with either foot.

18

constant practice. The versions of the kicks you will learn for basic self-defense are easier and more useful. Only experts can execute the spectacular kicks; almost anyone can learn and use the practical kicks.

Both the stamp kick and the side-snap kick allow you to stay well out of fist range of your adversary while you stop his intended attack. These kicks deliver power even when the person using them is not particularly strong or big. As noted earlier, most people have more muscle in their legs than in their arms.

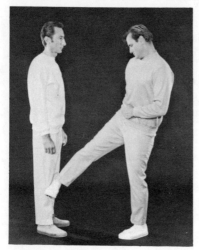

19

SIDE-SNAP KICK

19. The side-snap kick is made with the edge of your shoe. Facing your partner, turn your non-kicking foot at a 45° angle. This is a practice procedure for beginners; later in the course you will practice this kick from different starting positions. Draw your knee up and then kick sharply outward with the edge of your shoe. Keep out of arm's reach. Do not make contact on your partner. Practice using alternate right and left foot blows. Work toward maintaining good balance.

TOE KICK

20. This is an easier kick to learn, but it is not as useful as the two preceding kicks. More precision is required to apply the toe kick and it does not deliver as much force as the stamp or the side-snap.

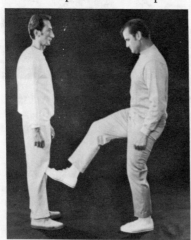

20   21

21. If you are wearing soft shoes or are barefoot, the toe kick is not practical; it would be more effective and safer to kick with the ball of the foot.

The correct action for the stamp kick is a smashing blow with follow through. For the side-snap and toe kicks, use whipping actions with recoil.

Practice procedures. Most training in the Oriental fighting arts is done barefoot. The custom developed because of cultural etiquette (the Japanese removed their shoes indoors), because much of the formal practice was done on a mat, and because sport forms are played barefoot. None of these reasons has application to modern self-defense.

For practical self-defense today, the only reason for working barefoot is for safety in beginning training. Kicks hurt; accidental contact can be painful.

When you have acquired enough skill to avoid accidental contact with your partner, practice at least part of the time with your shoes on. Even if your regular shoes are not very comfortable for this practice, you should wear them enough to get the feel of moving correctly in your street clothes. For street defense, it is unlikely that you would be wearing anything except your street clothes.

KICKING WITH POWER

You must never make contact when you practice kicking with your partner. To make contact and to practice full power kicks, you must have a suitable target. The experience of releasing full power when you kick is useful as a rehearsal of street defense.

The best targets for released-power kicks are a tackle dummy or blocking apparatus. If you do not have access to such equipment you can improvise a good kicking dummy by filling a duffle bag or laundry bag with sand and placing it against a wall. Do not try to suspend a kicking dummy unless you have a reinforced beam and heavy chain; a sand-filled bag is very heavy and it is not safe to hang one unless you are certain that the stress can be borne.

Whether you kick at a tackle dummy or your improvised kicking equipment, keep your kicks fairly low. The highest kick you need for practical defense is the knee-height of an average adult man. The best defense kicks are those aimed at the knee and shin.

WHERE TO HIT—BODY TARGET AREAS

For practical self-defense, you need only learn those body target areas which are most vulnerable, easiest to hit and most often available.

You should know the difference between target areas which are suitable when defending against vicious attack and where to hit when the attack is not serious.

Self-defense is for protection, not punishment. Every individual has the right to protect himself, but he does not have the right to punish! When the individual takes it upon himself to dispense punishment, or to take revenge, he is escalating violence and lawlessness.

The most effective target areas for self-defense are not necessarily those which are the most vulnerable to serious injury, but those which are most vulnerable to pain. You are quite justified in injuring an attacker if no other choice is available to you, but you are not justified in inflicting greater damage than is called for in any particular situation. No self-respecting person would choose to use a technique which causes serious or permanent injury if he could defend himself effectively with less force.

In traditional styles of unarmed fighting, many target areas are taught which are altogether unsuitable for basic self-defense. The famous chop to the back of the neck is a good example: it is highly unlikely that a person of slight build and moderate defense proficiency could hit a larger, strong person at the back of the neck with any degree of effectiveness. A heavy strong person hitting a smaller opponent at the base of the neck with force might do serious harm.

Choice of a body target will also depend on your space relationship to the adversary. Targets which are useful if you are in close should be used only if you cannot avoid being in that close to him. Don't step in to hit at any target if you can choose to hit from out of range of his hands.

RESULTS OF BLOWS

The descriptions of target areas will assume that a person of moderate skill is making the blow against an adversary who is of equal size or larger. If blows are struck into the same areas by a large, strong person against a smaller person, the result would be quite different. The result of a blow struck by a highly trained, experienced person would be very different from that of a person with basic or moderate skill.

There is always danger of injury if a powerful blow is struck, no matter what style of fighting is used. There has been so much nonsense printed about the "deadly" blows of karate and the Oriental weaponless fighting skills, that it tends to be forgotten that a powerful blow delivered by a skilled boxer could be fatal.

Precise, accurate descriptions of the result of any blow cannot be made without taking into consideration the strength, skill and accuracy of the person delivering the blow and the body build, state of health and emotional condition of the person being hit.

Practice procedure: Touch the target areas lightly to help you memorize them; simulate blows to the target areas without making contact.

FRONT UPPER BODY TARGETS

22. Nose.   The top of the nose is a good close-in target. It does not take a power blow to hurt and disconcert an adversary by hitting onto the nose. A slash is appropriate for striking across the top of the nose.

Up under the nose, a heel-of-palm blow or slash could be used.

23. Side of neck.   The open-hand slash can be used into either side of the neck. This is an area sensitive to pain, but it would take a forceful blow by a strong person to cause serious or permanent injury.

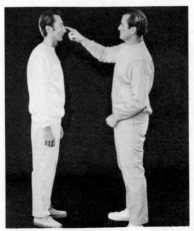

22   23

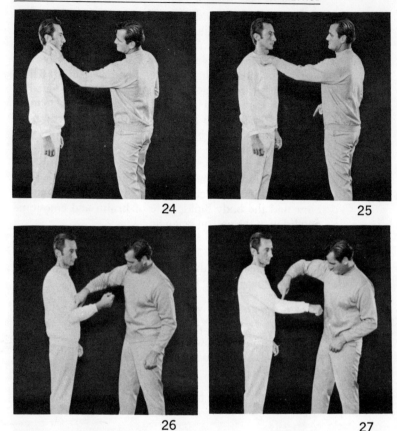

24

25

26

27

24. Ear.   Just behind the ear lobe is an area quite sensitive to pain. A slashing open-hand blow at the ear lobe,
will reach the correct target area.

25. Shoulder muscle.   At the base of the neck where it
joins the shoulder is a prominent muscle structure. A
downward slash onto the shoulder close to the neck is
the most effective blow. There is little possibility of
injury unless the blow is delivered with great force, but
a moderate blow can cause considerable pain and
numbness.

26. Bend of elbow.   A slashing blow struck into the
crook of the elbow is effective because it could bend his
arm and cause pain.

27. Forearm.   At the mound of the forearm there is a
vulnerable area which can be struck with a slashing hand
blow. To locate it, turn your own arm so that the forearm mound is pronounced; squeeze it with your thumb
until you find the area where pain is produced. A quick,
snappy blow to this target could numb the arm.

Practice Procedure

Touch all the target areas you have just learned: the nose, both ear lobes, both sides of the neck, both elbows, both forearms. This is to help you remember that your target is not just on one side.

Now, simulate all the blows you could make to these target areas and do them first with one hand and then the other. Make cross-body blows as well as outward and inward blows.

Then, simulate double-handed, simultaneous blows by striking into both sides of your partner's neck at once and by striking down onto both his forearms at one time. *DO NOT MAKE CONTACT*. Work slowly.

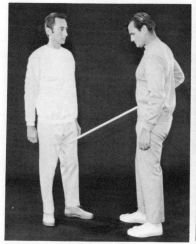 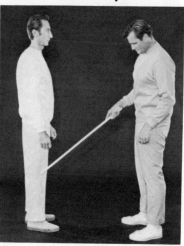

28   29

28. Upper thigh.   A kick into the upper thigh can cause pain and might numb the leg. It is not an ideal target but there are times and situations in which it could be effective to use a knee kick into the upper thigh.

I do not regard the groin as a suitable target area for self-defense. Most men would automatically protect the groin. There is no reason to use a vicious groin kick for self-defense if any other defense action would be effective. In order to kick into the groin, it is necessary to come in very close to your assailant; unless you are already close, it is not prudent to move in close to begin your defense.

29. Knee.   I consider the knee an ideal target. It is vulnerable; it is often available; you can kick into the knee without coming into fist range of your adversary.

Even a moderately forceful kick into the knee will cause considerable pain. It is possible to take your adversary off balance or even put him on the ground with a kick into the knee.

A stamping kick delivers greatest force, but you could use a side-snap kick. A kick directly into the front of the knee is effective, but more effective is a kick aimed at a 45 degree angle at the side of the kneecap.

30

30. Shin. On most people, the shin is peculiarly sensitive to pain. A snappy kick with the edge of your shoe or a stamping kick into the shin is a very effective, practical defense action.

A toe kick is effective, but requires greater precision than the side-snap and stamp kicks.

Practice Procedure

In slow motion, and without making contact, go through the actions of kicking into both legs, both knees and both shins of your partner. Simulate all the kicks you have learned to the target areas of the leg.

COMBINING ACTIONS

Now that you have learned some "words" in your basic vocabulary of defense, you will combine them into actions against some common attacks. Throughout this course you will be given examples of defenses, all of which are made by combining a relatively small group of actions.

Avoid the habit of thinking of a defense action as limited to the specific example which is known. Think of other situations in which the same defense might be appropriate. Think of other combinations of the actions which could be appropriate.

Combination Heel-of-Palm Blow and Slash—Defense Example

Many attacks begin with a reaching action. The specific intent does not matter. If the hand comes forward, whether it is to grip, slash, push or pull, you could use the defense which follows. (Against a fast jab this would not be the most appropriate defense.)

31.   As his arm moves forward, strike it cross-body with a thrusting heel-of-palm blow.

32, 33.   Follow with a back-handed slash into the side of his neck.

31

32

33

34

35

Combination Slash, Kick & Heel-of-Palm Blow

This is another example of a combination of actions you have already learned. Again, the attack begins with a reaching hand, not a fast jab; specific intent is not significant.

34.   As he reaches, slash down onto the forearm of his reaching hand.

35.   Then, simulate a heel-of-palm blow up under his chin and kick into his shin.

Front Two-Handed Reach—Defense Example

In this example, your partner simulates a two-handed reach. The specific intent is not significant; you are reacting to the two hands reaching out to grab, choke, pull or push.

36.   Your partner simulates two-handed reach. You slash down into his elbows with vigor.

37.   Follow with a heel-of-palm blow up under his chin.

36   37

STAY OUT OF REACH / MAINTAIN BALANCE

It is not an automatic reaction to respond correctly to the threat of attack. Even very simple actions must be learned and performed a few times to make them available to you in an emergency.

Stay Out of Reach

38.   Your partner simulates a reaching attack to which you respond by stepping *back* and kicking into his shin or knee. Even if you could take just a short step back, you would be out of arms' reach. Leaning your upper body away from him increases the distance from his reaching hands.

38

39   40

Maintain Balance

39, 40.   The correct response to being grabbed and pushed is *not* pushing back. If you have allowed yourself to be grabbed in the manner shown, and are losing your balance backward, take a step *back* to regain your balance and kick with the other foot.

Practice both these procedures, but concentrate on the first one. Prevention is the best part of defense.

BLOCKING BLOWS—A Practice Procedure

In street defense, it is highly unlikely that you would have to block more than one or two blows. The practice procedure which follows is designed to develop response. In this lesson, you need only block correctly; it is not necessary to work quickly. When you have developed the ability to respond to the direction of the oncoming fist, then you work to increase speed of reaction.

41.   Start from standing position; your partner simulates obvious intention to punch. In this situation you can see which fist will come forward and be ready to block it.

42.   As he punches, block his forearm with a vigorous slash.

43.   He then simulates a second punch with the other hand; block that with a slashing hand blow.

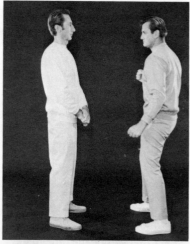

41

42.

43.

Repeat this practice until you can block the blow correctly, hitting the forearm for greatest efficiency. Then practice it with the one-two punches coming in different order—right, left, left, right—so that your response is not rigid.

COMBINING ACTIONS FOR COMPLETE DEFENSE

In this first lesson you have learned the actions for making a number of defenses. By combining the actions, by continuing the actions as necessary, by varying the order of the actions, you should be able to carry on complete defenses against a variety of forward attacks. The example which follows is only one of the possible combinations of material you have learned. Practice this one as shown; then practice variations of your own.

Start with your partner simulating threat of attack.

44. As he punches, kick into his knee.

45. Block both his arms.

46. Apply a hand blow.

After you have practiced this defense example, practice variations of your own invention. Develop flexibility by using the different hand and foot blows you have learned and by using alternately right and left hand and foot blows.

Do not try to work quickly but concentrate on smooth transition from one technique to another so that your defense is continuous. When you can work smoothly and continuously (without stopping to think what comes next) that will be the time to increase speed.

44

45

46

BLOCKING FOUR BLOWS—A Practice Procedure

This procedure is a progression from the blocking which you practiced in Lesson #1. Blocking two blows should be sufficient for street defense. Practice of blocking four blows is to improve reaction timing.

47.   Block a right hand blow with an upward and outward slash, using your left hand.

48.   Block a left high blow, up and out with your right hand.

49.   Block a low right blow, downward and outward with a left-handed slash.

50.   Block a left, low blow with your right hand.

47

48

49

50

For timing, count 1, 2, 3, 4 as you block the blows. The practice procedure is for smooth and correct response. The count of 1, 2, 3, 4, should be rhythmical, speeding up as your ability to react improves. Then, practice this procedure with the blows mixed up, high and low, left and right.

HAND BLOWS

I do not regard conventional boxing blows as appropriate for practical self-defense. Naturally, a skilled boxer can use them effectively; of course, a heavy, big man could punch with great efficiency. But a smaller, moderately skilled man defending himself against a heavier, larger man is at a considerable disadvantage trying to use boxing blows—reach and power being the critical factors.

If, however, you already know boxing blows and feel comfortable and confident using them, they can be combined with the other techniques in this course to good advantage. Because it is almost automatic to draw back from a blow aimed into the face, a punch can be used as a feint, or into the face to cause pain and disorientation.

51

PUNCHING

51.   The karate type punching technique is more useful for street defense than the conventional boxing punch. In boxing, it is assumed that the whole hand delivers the power. In the karate punch, the striking point is the flat of the two large knuckles, increasing the penetration force of the blow; less power is required for an effective blow. Only the face, particularly the nose, is a suitable target for the straight-out punch (in basic self-defense).

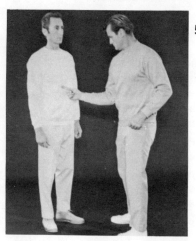

52. A punch into the middle section of a heavier man is only effective if delivered in an upward direction at the point shown. The target is just below where the ribs part and above the belt line.

53. An upward punch, palm up, can cause considerable pain. This blow is only for use when you are already close in; do not step in to deliver this blow unless you have already stopped the intended attack.

SIDE OF FIST

54. The side of the fist can be used for head blows. If you strike back-handed into the side of the head, it is jarring. You can hit with the side of your fist without hurting your knuckles.

55. A smashing side-fist blow down onto the nose is extremely painful and disconcerting.

KICKS & TARGETS

INSIDE EDGE OF SHOE

56.   This kick is not as versatile as the snap-kick using the outside edge of your shoe, but it is appropriate and useful in some situations. If you are very close (closer than is shown in the photo) you might find it easier to kick with the inside edge. The action is snappy; the target is the shin.

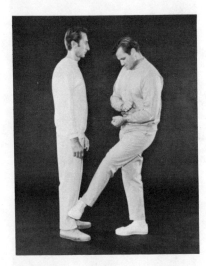

56

SNAP-KICK, SCRAPE & STAMP

57.   An effective and easy combination of kick, scrape and stamp is a useful series of actions for close-in defense. The action begins with a side-snap into the shin.

58.   Scrape down the length of the shin.

59.   Stamp down onto the instep.

60.   The vulnerable part of the foot is the top of the arch.

61, 62.   The ankle bone is sensitive and often unprotected. Kick with the inside or outside edge of the shoe.

57

58

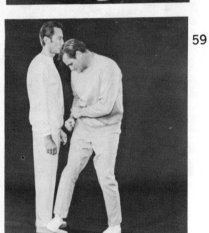

59

60

61

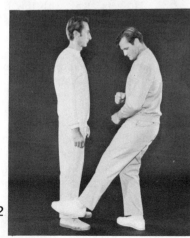

62

NUISANCE SITUATIONS

There are some situations which could hardly be classed as attacks, but they are annoying or humiliating and you should know how to deal with them. Your reaction has to be appropriate to the seriousness of intent. You would certainly not be justified in treating this as a vicious attack or in applying a defense which would only be justified against a vicious attack.

63

64

THE LEANER

63. He gets away with this behavior because he feels physically superior or he thinks that you are intimidated by him.

64. Place your fingers at the side of his neck; place your thumb into the hollow of his throat (below the adam's apple) and *gently* press.

You are not trying to provoke a fight. As you apply the thumb press, just say something to the effect that you don't want to be leaned on. The combination of your physical action and your calm statement should make clear your intention not to be bullied.

When you practice this with your partner, be very careful not to jab your thumb into the hollow; it is extremely painful.

65   66

65.   An alternative to the thumb press is—jab your
knuckle up under his last rib. Above the waist, just
under the ribs, there is a spot which is quite sensitive to
pain, on most people, 66.

FRONT CHOKE DEFENSES
In this course, you will learn more than one possible response to the common types of attacks which you might
encounter. You should practice all the techniques shown.
Later in the course, you will begin to select from among
the techniques those which you can do more easily and
comfortably and which you prefer. Following are two of
the possible front choke breaks. They might also be used
against two-handed reaching or two-handed shoulder
grab.

CLASPED-HAND THRUST

Your partner simulates the front choke by gripping your
shoulders. He should take a firm grip.

67.   Clasp your hands together (do not intertwine your
fingers) and start the action low, as shown.

68, 69.   With a vigorous upward thrust, bring your
clasped hands up between his arms to break his grip. The
action must be quick and thrusting, not pushing.

70.   Continue by smashing down onto his nose with
your clasped hands.

Kick into the shin.

When defending against a choke, it is essential to relieve
the pain first, by weakening or breaking the grip.

Practice the same defense as a response to the *attempt* to
apply a choke. Develop the habit of responding as the
attempt is made; you don't have to wait for an attack to
be completed before you start your defense.

67

68

69

70

CROSS-HAND BREAK

Your partner simulates choke by gripping your shoulders
firmly.

71, 72, 73. The two actions which break the grip follow each other quickly. The action is a jerky, snappy
palm blow, struck as close to his wrist as possible. Strike
first at one wrist and then the other. Avoid a pushing action. It is the snap and jerk action which breaks the grip,
rather than power.

74. Deliver simultaneous slashing blows (cross-hand-
ed) into the sides of his neck.

In practicing with your partner, repeat the breaking
action until you can do it properly. Then simulate the actions of continuing the defense using hand and foot blows,
as necessary.

71

72

73

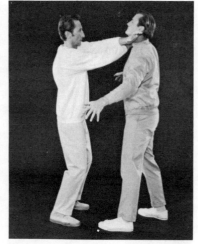

74

OFFENSE/DEFENSE: Which is Which?

Techniques, in themselves, are neither defensive nor offensive. You can use a fist blow to defend yourself, but the same fist blow could be used to start a fight.

A style of fighting is neither defensive nor offensive. There are offensive and defensive tactics in all styles of fighting, but even within the offensive/defensive category, both opponents could be using similar styles of blows.

The aggressor is defined not in terms of his fighting style, but in terms of his attitude. If someone starts a fight, or insists on fighting, if you do not want to fight, he is clearly the aggressor and you are clearly defending yourself.

Don't Take the Bait

Merely because someone challenges to fight does not mean that you have to accept the challenge. If you do not want to fight, do everything you can to avoid fighting. Have the courage of your convictions! Don't cower or grovel; don't behave as though you are incapable of taking care of yourself. Make it clear that you *choose* not to fight. When you cannot avoid a fight—defend with spirit. If it is obvious that the aggressor means to force a fight, refuses to allow you to decline to fight, then you are justified in stopping him before he can hit you.

READY STANCES

75. You are threatened, or challenged.

76. Take a step back, if you can. If you are out of his fist range, you have a better chance to decline to fight.

75

76

What you say in this situation may determine whether or not you have to defend yourself. If you are prepared to handle this threat, you might talk your way out of it. Unless you can give some thought to it beforehand, you are not likely to stay calm enough to control yourself. What you say should be said in a non-hostile tone of voice. Tell him that you do not want to fight.

Your stance is obviously nonbelligerent, yet you are able to move into action quickly. Take a T-position for good balance. Your hands are open, ready to strike, but not signalling intention to fight. (Making a fist signals intent to fight.)

When to Hit First

77.   The other man is clearly the aggressor. You have stated that you don't want to fight; your stance is neutral. If he cannot be dissuaded from fighting, you are justified in striking the first blow in response to his *intended* attack. You don't have to get hit before you start your defense. As he moves in, kick, hit and YELL. Continue with hand and foot blows as necessary. The double striking action, combined with a loud yell, could be enough to stop him.

78.   An alternate ready stance which does not show hostility is this one. Your striking hand is held in front of you, open, with your other hand covering it, as shown. Push out with your striking hand and pull back with the other hand to create a spring tension. You are ready to strike and kick as in 77.

77   78

79

79.   Another possible ready stance which does not signal readiness to fight is with your arms folded. In this
stance you are creating a spring tension by pulling back
with one arm as you push forward with the other. You
are prepared, if necessary, to strike and kick as in 77.

DEFENSE AGAINST FIST FIGHTER

Example of Combination of Techniques Against Close-In Attack

Most of the students who have had defense training from
me (in personal instruction and through my books) report that they have had less trouble after their training
than before. They encounter fewer occasions to fight partly because they are more aware of how to avoid fights,
partly because they feel more confident about declining
to fight (without losing face), and partly because their
positive behavior discourages the bully. Bullies want victims, not adversaries.

Those students who have had to defend themselves are
surprised that one or two actions are usually enough to
stop a fight. A street fight is not a contest, and it is possible that the first one or two actions of an orderly, spirited, effective defense will finish such an attack.

However, to give you the confidence to handle street attack, you should learn and practice a complete, ongoing
series of actions so that you feel competent to deal with
an assailant who might not be stopped with the first blow.
The following is a practice procedure to develop your
ability to continue the defense for longer than might ever
be necessary on the street.

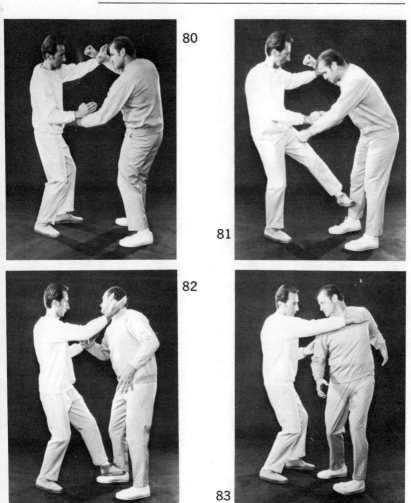

First, practice the sequence as shown.

80. Stop two blows with slashing open-hand blows.

81. Kick into the knee or shin.

82. While he is hurt and distracted by the kick, strike an open-hand blow into the neck.

Repeat the kicks and hand blows several times before you continue to the next action, which is new.

83. When you have weakened and hurt your assailant with hand and foot blows, spin him around by thrusting sharply back at his left shoulder as you slap his right shoulder forward with your left hand. The action to twist him around must be vigorous and snappy.

84

84. Continue hand and foot blows as necessary to subdue the assailant. The body target areas, for this practice, will be the side of the neck and the back of the knee.

As you work through this series of actions, try to develop smooth, continuing hand and foot blows, rather than speed. When you can progress from one blow to another without hesitation, you can practice to increase speed.

After you can do the series shown, vary the hand and foot blows, using your full repertoire of types of blows and alternate left and right hand and foot blows for greatest efficiency.

FIGHTING STANCES—Uses & Limitations

It is not always prudent or possible to assume a fighting stance for self-defense. A fighting stance is out of the question for defense against a back attack. If a fast punch is coming your way it would be ludicrous to take a fighting stance before trying to evade or stop the punch.

In the movies, a karate fighter always take a weird fighting stance because it is an exotic and dramatic pose. It is done that way because it looks good for the camera, not because it is practical.

In training for karate contest there is heavy emphasis on fighting stances because stances *are* important in tournament. Tactics which are appropriate for contest are not the appropriate tactics for street defense. Emphasizing stances for street defense confuses the applications of sport and self-defense tactics.

Most sensible men would rather avoid a fight than fight on the street. Taking a fighting stance is a signal of willingness to fight. Once you take a fighting stance, you are committed to the fight.

When a fighting stance is possible, you should consider the psychological and physical factors. If you think you have a chance of avoiding the fight, don't take a fighting stance.

Both fighting stances which follow are adequate for self-defense. They minimize the body target you present to your adversary. Both give good, strong balance. You can make hand and foot blows easily from either stance.

85   86

85.   The conventional boxing stance has the advantage of masking the style of your defense. From this stance, the adversary might expect only conventional fist blows.

86.   This stance is unconventional, gives a somewhat better high guard and it could disconcert an adversary who might feel unable to cope with an unconventional style of fighting. Take a T-position with your strong hand forward.

Ordinarily, a boxer guards with his left up (if he is right-handed). I advise taking the karate stance with your strong hand forward. Though you should practice hand blows with either hand, you should be prepared to deliver your first hand blow with your favored hand. Unless you are trained and are in physical condition to go the distance, you had better end the fight quickly!

Your lead hand is ready to deliver a slash. You can hold your other hand open or fisted, as you prefer. By shifting your weight slightly onto your rear foot, you can deliver a good kick without loss of balance.

FINGER STABS

Target areas for finger stabs are the soft, fleshy parts of the body.

87.   The correct basic position for finger stabs is shown. Fingers are held together, your hand is slightly cupped, thumb is held flat against the index finger. The action is jabbing.

88.   The blow can be delivered straight forward.

89.   Finger stabs can be made upward, palm up.

90.   Finger stabs can be delivered straight out or downward, palm down.

91.   Against moderately serious attack, close-in stab into the neck, onto the prominent muscle (sterno mastoid) which you can feel when you turn your neck. A sharp jab into this area is very painful, but not serious.

92.   Up under the jaw is a target for finger stabs; painful but not serious.

93, 94.   A finger stab into the hollow of the throat or onto the windpipe can be extremely painful and dangerous. In the event of vicious, close-in attack, you could be justified in striking at this area, or into the eyes.

87   88

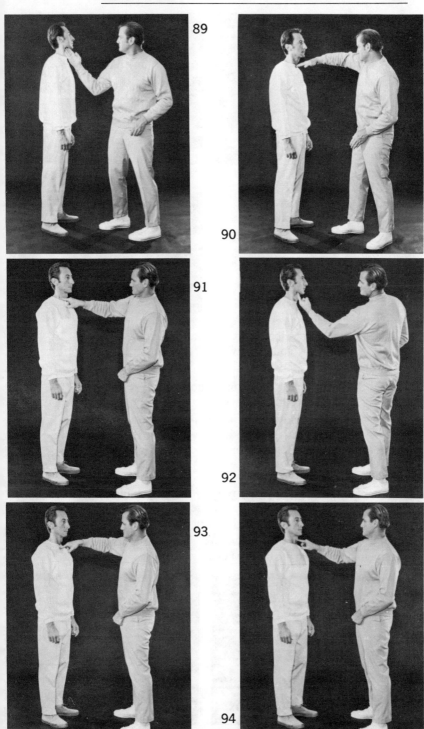

95

96

97

FOREARM BLOW

95.   You must be close in to apply a forearm blow, but it is a strong blow and effective where appropriate. You can strike upward, as though hitting into the face.

96.   A forearm blow can be made downward, as though hitting onto the forearm.

97.   A forearm blow struck at the nerve just above the wrist can be effective. The advantage of striking into this target is that you do not have to come in so close.

ELBOW BLOW

98.   This is an effective, strong blow, only limited in use because you must be in very close to deliver it. It can be an upward blow, as though hitting up under the chin.

99.   An elbow blow can be circular, from side to side, as though hitting into the face or head.

98

99

LESSON FOUR

KICKING PRACTICE PROCEDURES

The procedures which follow are meant to develop proficiency and technique. The kicks are the ones you learned in the first lesson.

FORWARD STAMP

To develop technique for the forward stamp, practice raising your knee high and then stamping forward with vigor. Do not make contact, but aim at the knee and at the upper thigh for reference target. Practice alternate right and left foot blows.

100.   Raise your knee high.

101.   Stamp forward with the bottom of your foot.

Practice to improve your balance; practice to release all of your potential power; practice delivering several kicks in succession.

100

101

SIDE SNAP

102.   Practice the side-snap kick by raising your knee and positioning your kicking foot cross-body.

103.   From the exaggerated position shown in 102, snap outward vigorously, striking with the edge of your shoe. Aim at the shin as reference point. Do not make contact with your partner. Practice to develop kicking efficiency without loss of balance. Practice to deliver several side-snap kicks in succession with the same foot.

STAMP KICK

104.   Practice the stamping kick from the side by raising your knee high and then delivering a vigorous kick with the bottom of your shoe. Do not make contact.

For basic self-defense there is no special value in practicing high kicks. It is good exercise to practice high kicks and it can help you develop flexibility and improve balance, but you must remember that the abilities which are developed through such special exercises are maintained only if you continue to practice. The ability to deliver self-defense kicks does not require constant, ongoing practice. You need only learn to do them moderately well and they will be available for practical use.

REAR BODY TARGETS

105. Side of neck.   The side of the neck is a target from the rear as well as from the front or side. The slash is the most efficient hand blow; delivered cross-body, palm down; from the outside, palm up.

I do not regard the back of the neck as a suitable target for basic defense. It is awkward to reach on a larger person; power is needed for effect. It works very well in the movies because the stuntman is paid to fall down when he gets chopped!

106. Shoulder muscle.   The shoulder muscle at the base of the side of the neck can be struck with a downward slash.

107. Kidney.   The only mid-body rear target which might be considered suitable for basic defense is the kidney. It is a limited target because a smaller person with moderate ability and moderate strength cannot expect to do more than jar or cause discomfort to a heavier, bigger man. Striking into the kidney area is more efficient than hitting at the upper back.

102.

103

104

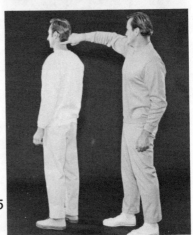

105

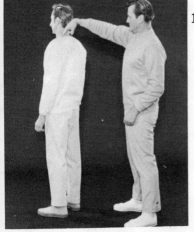

106

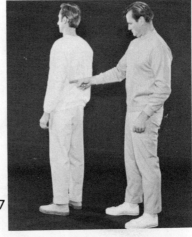

107

108. Upper thigh.   A kick into the upper thigh is painful and could knock an adversary down.

109. Back of knee.   Kicking into the back of the knee is effective and easier than kicking higher. It is a better target than kicking into the upper thigh because it is easier to take an assailant down by kicking sharply into the knee to bend his leg. This is my favored back body target.

110. Calf.   A forceful kick into the calf causes pain and could immobilize the leg temporarily.

111. Achilles' tendon.   Just above the heel, there is a prominent tendon which is vulnerable to a vigorous kick.

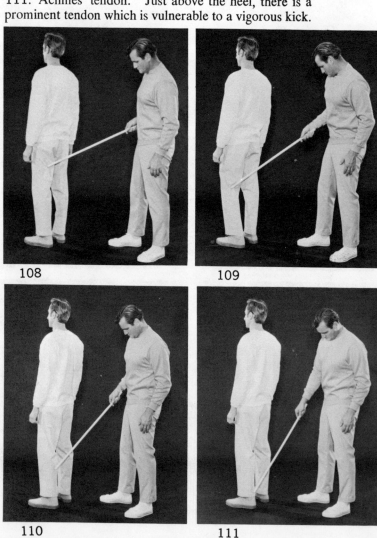

108

109

110

111

112

113

MORE NUISANCE SITUATIONS
RESPONSE TO SHOULDER PUNCH

Another jolly nuisance is the shoulder puncher or back slapper.

112.   He often makes a habit of greeting you with a heavy hand.

113.   Slash at his arm with vigor to let him know you don't like being treated this way.

If you want to break his bad habit without offending him, follow up your slash with an apology for hurting him. He can't really be angry with you for reacting to his punch, but he won't be likely to do it again.

114

115

RESPONSE TO SHOULDER BUMP

114.   The shoulder bump might be done in a joking manner, or it could be intended to humiliate.

115.   You can grind your heel onto the top of his instep.

116

117

118

119

120

RESPONSES TO HAND SQUEEZE

Three possible ways of dealing with the jolly hand-squeezer are shown.

116. He is not trying to injure you, but showing off his superior strength.

117. You can grind down onto the top of his forearm with the bony underside of your forearm. The top of the forearm is much more sensitive than the under side, so you don't hurt your arm as you apply this action.

118. Or, you can effect release by pressing his thumb back at the first joint. Push at his thumb with the heel of your palm.

119. With your extended knuckle, grind into the top of his hand, at the area shown in 120.

A fourth way of dealing with this situation is to step on his instep. Any of the preceding actions could be effective. Choose one or two; you won't have to remember all of them.

WRIST-GRIP RELEASES

If your wrist is gripped by a larger stronger adversary, you cannot expect to effect release by pulling straight back.

ONE-HAND GRIP

121. As you kick into his shin to divert him, slash down onto his gripping arm.

122. Make a fist of your captured hand and grip it with your free hand; push outward.

121   122

123

124

125

123.   His normal reaction to your outward push will be a pull inward. Take advantage of his movement and draw your hand free, pulling it out from between his thumb and forefinger. Study the photos to see the difference between pulling straight back (which would be pulling against the strong part of his grip) and pulling free at the weakest part. If you pull straight back, his whole hand opposes your pull; if you pull across, only his fingers oppose your action.

124.   Free your captured hand; use snappy, cross-body action.

125.   Hit with the released hand.

In order to be effective, the release must be preceded by kicks to distract and hurt your adversary.

TWO-HAND GRIP

This technique for release from a two-hand grip is essentially the same as the foregoing technique. Because a double-handed grip is stronger, you will have to rely to a great extent on hurting him with several kicks into the shin before you attempt to free your captured wrist.

126.   After several vigorous kicks, make a fist of your captured hand and reach over and between his arms to grip your own fist. Push down to get him to react by pulling up.

127.   Assisted by his upward movement, pull your captured hand free, jerking it up and cross-body. Continue with hand and foot blows, as necessary.

126   127

RESTRAINTS

The intelligent thing to do, after you have stopped an intended attack, is to escape. There are few instances in which it is sensible for the average person to restrain an adversary.

In this course, you will learn only minimum restraint techniques as preparation for the emergency in which it could be appropriate or necessary to control a subdued opponent. The arm bar is to be applied after stopping an intended attack.

128

129

BASIC ARM BAR

128. After stopping the attack with hand and foot blows, grip his wrist with your right hand and slash at his arm with your left hand.

129. Turn his arm so that the back of his elbow is up. Place the under side of your forearm at the back of his elbow. Apply pressure by pressing down with your forearm onto his elbow as you pull upon on his captured wrist. For serious attack, it is appropriate to *smash* down onto the elbow with a forearm blow.

130. You can take him down to the ground by continuing to apply pressure.

130

BACKWARD BLOWS

Of the hand and arm blows, the two most practical for striking to the rear are the open-hand slash and the elbow blow. These should be practiced with reference to the target area. Do not make contact. In beginning practice of backward blows, stand further away from your partner than is shown in the photos.

OPEN-HAND BLOW

131, 132.   Without moving your feet, turn your head, look at your target and slash back into the side of the neck or head. You must turn your head to see what you are hitting. Seeing your target is more efficient than striking blindly. Practice turning and hitting to either side.

131   132

ELBOW BLOW

From close in, the elbow blow is particularly effective and practical for hitting to the rear.

133.   Hit around and back, into the side of the head.

134.   Hit up, under the chin.

135.   Strike back into the abdomen.

Choice of target area for the elbow will depend partly on the relative sizes of the people. Against an adversary of about equal size, you might use the head or face as target; against an adversary considerably larger, the mid-section could be a better target. An elbow blow struck in an upward direction at the base of the sternum could deliver considerable force into the internal organs.

KICKING—Back

The two kicks which are most efficient for hitting backward at an adversary are the side-snap and the stamp. The kicks should be kept low; the target area is from the knee down. Higher kicks can be done by those who are highly trained and who maintain skill with practice; for basic defense they are not practical.

136.   Turn your head to look at your target; stamp back into the knee or shin. Turn your foot so that it is horizontal and makes the full length of your shoe the possible striking point.

Kicking in this way requires less precision than a kick with your toe pointed down. Practice to acquire equal proficiency with right and with left foot. Deliver the kick without moving your non-kicking foot, but be certain to turn your head to see where you are kicking.

137.   Turn your head, deliver side-snap kick into shin.

138.   The side-snap may be followed with a scraping down the shin and finish with a stamp onto the instep.

Practice to develop equal proficiency with right and left foot. Practice alternate right and left foot kicks.

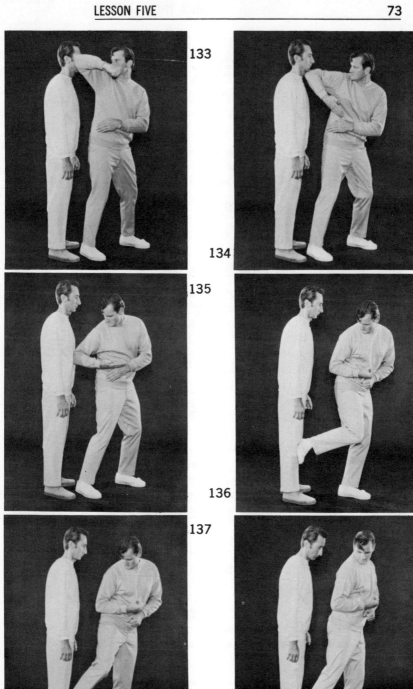

133

134

135

136

137

138

139

139. As a practice procedure, stand well out of reach of your partner and deliver stamping kicks back. Practice to avoid loss of balance. Practice to extend the range of your kick.

Do not make contact. Use your partner as a target reference point.

RESPONSE TO THREAT OF BACK ATTACK

The premise of this course is that defense is as much prevention as it is preparation to cope with physical attack. Part of prevention is the ability to recognize potentially threatening situations and in such situations to be more alert to subtle signs of danger.

Recognition of possible danger is partly a matter of judgment and partly a matter of experience. You would almost certainly be safer from threat of attack in the company of friends on a well-lit, familiar street in your own neighborhood than you would be alone, on a dark street in a strange place. There are bizarre exceptions, of course, but we are talking about what is likely and common.

If you are in a place which seems to be dangerous, be prepared to respond to clues which give a warning before an attack is actually completed. It is especially important to be alert to threat of back attack because you are more vulnerable if your adversary is behind you.

Practice Procedure

Preparation to defend against possible back attack means readiness to respond to the threat before an attack has been completed. The cues to which you should be able to react are: sight, sound and touch. In the following procedure, you will practice reacting to light touch, faint sounds and the sight of movement.

140.   Your partner signals the threat by touching you very lightly on the shoulder, by reaching, as shown in 141, or by stepping or sliding his foot so that you hear his footstep.

142.   Your response to any of these cues is: without moving your feet, turn your head as you slash, as shown. This is a protective slash.

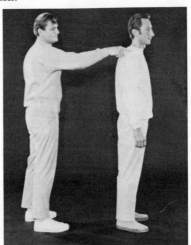

140

141

142

143.   After you have practiced the look and slash and can respond fairly quickly to the "danger" cue, practice the next phase of response. At the cue, take a step *away from* (not around to) the adversary, turn your head to see what you are hitting, deliver simultaneous slash and kick. By taking a step forward, rather than around, you place yourself further out of his reach as you go into action. If you step too far away to hit him, he is too far away to hit you, too.

144.   Then, turn and face him. Continue with hand and foot blows, as necessary.

BACK TAKEDOWN

Judo throws are not practical for self-defense. They require greater skill than can be maintained by the average person. Dr. Kano, the founder of judo, did not intend that judo should be used for self-defense. The throws and falls of sport judo were designed for body development and physical education.

For basic self-defense, you need only learn a few simple ways of taking an opponent to the ground. The takedowns are useful as ending techniques, after you have stopped the intended attack and have hurt and weakened the adversary with hand and foot blows. Being put on the ground is more than physical defeat, it is psychological defeat. Before you practice the takedown, re-read the section on falling in the pre-instruction.

For this session, practice the takedown as an action which follows the spin-around, which you learned earlier.

145.   Spin your partner around.

146.   Reverse your hands, grip him at the back of the collar with your left hand and at the upper arm with your right hand.

147.   Push into the back of his (near) knee with your right foot as you pull back on his upper body with both hands. Stand out of the line of his fall as he goes down. He should fall over your leg, but not into your body.

Practice this in slow motion with your partner. It is not necessary to slam him on the ground to learn the proper way of effecting the takedown.

143

144

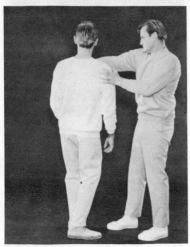

145

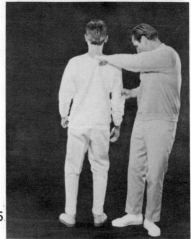

146.

147

COMPLETE, CONTINUING DEFENSE: Example Showing Combination of Kicks, Hand Blows, Spin and Takedown.

This is a more sophisticated combination of techniques for an ongoing defense, using techniques which you already know. Practice for smooth, flowing actions. When your work is continuous, without hesitation between the actions, practice to increase speed.

148, 149.   From out of fist range, kick twice into the knee. Deliver one kick and then turn and kick again.

150.   Block both his arms with slashes.

151.   Deliver another hand and foot blow simultaneously.

152.   Spin him around.

153.   Takedown.

148

149

150

151

152

153

LEAPING

Of the possible ways of avoiding an attack, leaping is one of the best. Against a rushing, oncoming attack, leaping out of the line of intended attack is a safe and efficient response. If there is space in which to move, you could put yourself in an advantageous position to defend and minimize the possibility of being hit by the assailant.

Moderate practice in leaping and occasional mental practice of this procedure will keep it available for you. Unless you are in very poor physical condition, you should be able to leap far enough.

154.   Your partner simulates a rushing forward attack, to which you respond by leaping to the outside of the attacking hand.

155.   In this position, you are least vulnerable to his attack.

Practice to leap lightly and without loss of balance.

154

155

LEAP & KICK

Combine the action of leaping with a kick which follows immediately.

156.   Your partner simulates a rushing punch. You leap to the outside of his punching hand and kick into the back of his knee. Practice this to right and left sides.

In this procedure speed is *essential*. As your partner cues you by taking a step forward, quickly leap and kick without hesitation.

LEAP, KICK, TAKEDOWN

This is another example of combination of actions for a complete, ongoing defense.

157.   As your partner simulates attack, leap to the outside of the punching hand and kick. Without hesitation, apply the takedown. For practice, you need only take your partner to off-balance, as shown.

KNIFE ATTACK—Defense Example

Do not attempt to grip, grab or grapple with a knife. A highly skilled, exceptionally proficient individual might be able to use an old-fashioned grappling technique as a knife defense, but there are more efficient defenses which could be used by individuals with moderate levels of skill.

If the knife is being used for intimidation, and the primary purpose is robbery, do not attempt to stop him. Only if the man really intends to use his knife and that is his *sole purpose* should you go into action. There is always some risk involved in opposing a knife-armed person; if the knife is not going to be used, don't take the risk. If the knife is surely going to be used, you must defend with spirit—there is no alternative.

158.   Your partner simulates knife attack. Note which hand holds the knife.

159.   Leap to the outside of the knife hand as he makes his move.

160.   Without hesitation, kick vigorously into the back of his knee.

161.   Immediately, grip his arm, *NOT* his hand or the knife, with both your hands and stiffen your arms to keep yourself away from the knife and continue to kick until he is weakened, subdued, or on the ground. Do not attempt to take the knife away from him. An armed man feels particularly helpless without his weapon and will resist its removal fiercely. Your objective is to hurt and immobilize him with kicks and escape as quickly as you can.

156

157

158

159

160

161

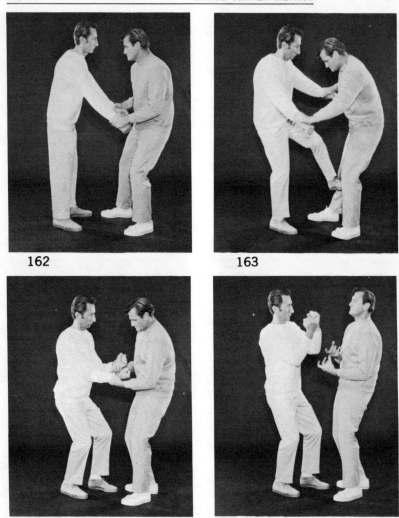

162

163

164

165

WRIST-GRIP RELEASE—Two Hands Gripping Both Wrists

The effectiveness of this defense depends upon vigorous, forceful kicks. In practice, obviously you are not going to make contact on your partner. Simulate snappy kicks; your partner should relax his grip somewhat as though to react to being kicked in the shin. This escape is a good defense action. You are not trying to prove that it works in your practice; you are simply learning it.

162.   Both wrists are gripped.

163.   As you kick sharply into the knee or shin, force your arms outward. The normal response to the outward movement is an inward push.

164.   Take advantage of his inward push; pull your arms sharply inward . . .

165.   and then up and out. Release is made at the weakest part of the grip, from between the thumbs and index fingers.

UNDER-ARM BODY GRAB DEFENSE

166.   You are gripped around the body, but your arms are free. Clasp your hands together (do not intertwine your fingers), turn your head to see where you are hitting. Hit into the side of the head or up under the chin with an elbow. His normal reaction would be to draw his head to the opposite direction; follow the first blow with another elbow blow to the opposite side. Continue hitting, and kick if necessary to effect release.

OVER-ARM BODY GRAB RELEASE

167.   You are gripped with your arms captured. Begin your defense with a vigorous kick into the shin. Even if you cannot see your leg target, if you turn your foot, some part of your shoe will hit the shin. As you kick, take a deep breath to expand his grip somewhat.

166   167

168

169

170

171

172

173

168.   Exhale sharply, as you drop down slightly, twist-ing your body quickly.

169.   Deliver an elbow blow into the midsection. If you are not fully released, continue kicking and use eblow blows until you are free. Then, turn to face your oppo-nent and continue hand and foot blows as necessary.

FRONT HEADLOCK—Release

170.   Front headlock has been effected. To relieve pres-sure, grip his arm at the wrist and forearm with both hands and jerk down; kick sharply onto his instep or into his shin. The *combination* of these actions, done sharply and vigorously, should be repeated until his grip is weak-ened.

171.   *After* hurting him and weakening his grip, take a step back behind him, maintaining your grip on his arm.

172.   Continue to grip his arm as you kick into the back of his knee.

173.   Or, pull his arm up behind his back for control. If control is appropriate, you can walk him from this posi-tion.

REVIEW SESSION

Before you continue, review everything you have learned in the course. It is assumed throughout the book that you have reasonable competence in a technique or procedure before you go on to the next technique. Your review here will have a new purpose; you will be getting ready to choose your individual repertoire of self-defense actions from among all those you have practiced.

As you review, you will be aware that you more readily choose one hand or foot blow, that you almost automati-cally favor certain combinations of actions. These fa-vored techniques are likely to be best and most efficient *for you.* Those techniques which you do not do as easily or as comfortably may not be suitable for you and you do not have to learn every single technique in this book for adequate basic self-defense. However, before you dis-card any particular technique as unsuitable or ineffective for you, make certain that you really understand it.

Continue to practice and use all the techniques shown in the course, even those you do not favor. At the end of the course, you can discard those you do not want and em-phasize, in mental practice, and in occasional physical practice, the performance of those you finally choose as your basic repertoire of defense actions.

FOREARM CHOKE FROM REAR—Defense & Escape

On TV and in the movies, the hero escapes from the choke shown in photo 174 by flipping the villain over his shoulder. Don't believe it. Throwing would be virtually impossible from this position; it would be absolutely impossible for the average person. In the movies, the over-the-shoulder stunt works because there is a stunt man paid to fall down. Real life is not like that. Go to the movies and watch television to be entertained—not for instruction.

The escape from this choke is similar to the escape from front headlock. Relief of the choking pressure is the essential first action.

174.   You are choked; pressure is against your windpipe; your balance is broken backward.

175.   Although you cannot expect to break the forearm choke with your hands, you can relieve the pressure and pain enough to allow you to continue effective defense. This is an important point; if you do not relieve the pressure, you might be unable to effect the escape. Grip his arm with both your hands and pull down with all your weight. Turn your head into the bend of his elbow to relieve pressure against your windpipe.

174

175

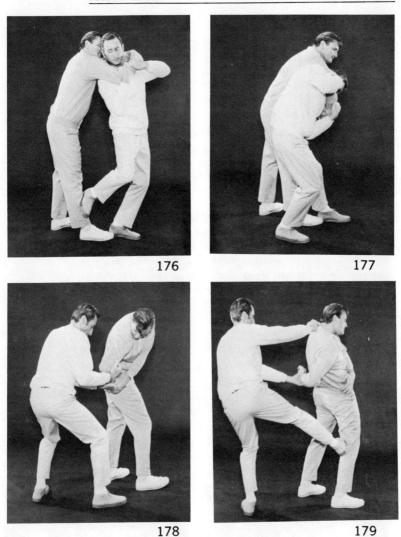

176

177

178

179

176. Maintaining your grip on his arm, kick with force into his shin or knee and continue kicking until you feel his grip has weakened.

177, 178. Only after you have loosened his grip, step back behind yourself and under his arm to effect escape. Do not push forward against his choking arm; that would increase pain and pressure. Stepping back allows you to effect release without forcing your throat against his forearm.

179. From this position you can effect a takedown, or restraint, whichever is appropriate.

PARRIES

Deflecting a blow is safer than opposing it. To grip or grapple with a punching fist requires great precision or superior strength, or both. Deflection allows you to avoid the intended blow.

HEEL-OF-PALM PARRY

180. The advantage of the heel-of-palm parry is that you can stay well away from your opponent as you deflect his blow with a snappy palm thrust. This is not a pushing action, nor a power action, but a fast, snappy thrust.

As you deflect the blow with the parry, duck your upper body out of fist range. As a practice procedure, take only one step to the outside of the attacking fist as you parry and duck your upper body out of range. The parry is useful when the situation does not permit leaping to evade an attack. Limiting yourself to one step is good practice to develop your ability to parry and duck efficiently in restricted space.

FOREARM PARRY

181. The forearm parry, which is characteristic of karate, has the advantage of being a strong parry, but has the disadvantage of bringing you in closer to your opponent. But, because it does not take great precision to use, it is often favored. In practice, allow yourself only a single step, duck your upper body out of range as far as you can. Apply the parry as a vigorous thrust, not as a push. Practice as a double parry, using both forearms.

180   181

182

183

DOUBLE-SLASH PARRY

182.   The double-slash parry is probably the least simple to learn and use of the three parries, but it is excellent if you can feel comfortable doing it. Using both hands gives the deflection more force; less precision is needed and a double guard is put up. Practice parrying left and right hand blows.

COMBINATION PARRY & TAKEDOWN—Against Fist Fighter

Your partner simulates intended fist attack.

183.   Take a short step to outside of punching arm and deflect it with a parry. A vigorous parry should turn him away from you somewhat.

184.   Slash to side of neck.

185.   Hit and kick; takedown if appropriate.

184

185

186

187

188

189

COMBINATION PARRY, ARM BAR—Defense Against
Back-Handed Club or Stick Attack

186.   A back-handed, swinging attack can be anticipated by the gesture. Holding the club or stick in the manner shown clearly indicates a swinging, back-handed attack.

187.   Step into the swinging arm. This is one of the very few instances in which you are safer in close. Because the club extends his striking range, you are less likely to be struck if you step in to block. Shown, is a double-forearm block.

188.   Grip his striking arm, not the weapon, as you kick with force into his knee.

189.   Apply the arm bar. Take him to the ground. Do not attempt to take away his weapon until he is completely subdued.

LEG & BODY TAKEDOWN

This is not a sport judo throw; it is a simplified self-defense adaptation of two judo throws combined. Observe the safety rules carefully.

Practice Procedure

This practice procedure is the best way of learning the fundamentals of the takedown. Follow the step-by-step instructions exactly. After you have learned the basics of the technique, you will be given examples of defense applications which will vary somewhat from the fundamental takedown.

190.   Partners face, within arms' reach. With your left hand grip his sleeve at about the elbow.

191.   Turn your left foot so that it points sharply at a right angle to your body. As you follow through to apply the takedown, most of your body weight will be on the left foot; unless weight is positioned correctly, you will lose your balance.

190   191

192

193

194

195

192.   Extend your right leg in front of his right leg as shown; start to put your right arm around his waist.

193.   Holding him firmly around the waist for safety, pull him into you and around and over your leg, using a twisting action of your arms and body. Support him as he goes down.

194.   When he is on the ground, take a step back with your right foot to get into strong balance.

195.   When you have learned the correct procedure for this takedown, practice it from the side of your partner, placing your arm around his body from the front, and tripping him over your extended leg, as shown. Twist

your upper body to effect the takedown; you are not trying to push him down with force, but are taking him off balance and around and down.

Support your partner so that he does not hurt himself. If you can do the takedown correctly to the point shown in the photo, you can do it properly.

COMBINATION LEAP, PARRY & TAKEDOWN

Practice combining a good leap and block with a takedown ending. Your leaping action should be fast, in response to your partner's cue of simulating a punch. The block and parry can be practiced as simultaneous actions; the takedown should follow without hesitation.

196.   Leap and block.

197.   From this position you are ready to apply a back takedown.

196   197

DEFENSES AGAINST KICKING ATTACKS

Because the leg is stronger than the arm, it is not efficient to try to grab, grapple with or block the kicking leg. If you cannot leap or step out of range of the intended attack, the most efficient technique for stopping the kick is deflection—a parry.

KNEE KICK DEFENSE

The knee kick is powerful, but a thrusting parry can divert the kick and put your opponent into awkward, off-balance position, or make him vulnerable for back takedown.

198, 199.   Using one or both hands, thrust his kicking knee away as you dodge your body out of range of his intended kick.

200.   Follow with appropriate hand and foot blows, as required. Finish with takedown, if appropriate.

HIGH KICK DEFENSE

The essential action of this defense is the same as for the defense against knee kick. Trying to catch the kicking leg is dangerous; deflecting it is easier and safer.

201.   Deflect the kicking leg in the direction which turns his back toward you.

202.   Continue with hand and foot blows; takedown if necessary.

TOE KICK DEFENSE

203.   He signals his intention by drawing his foot back.

198   199

200

201

202

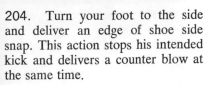

203

204. Turn your foot to the side and deliver an edge of shoe side snap. This action stops his intended kick and delivers a counter blow at the same time.

Apply additional hand and foot blows, as required. The foregoing is a very simple action, but it is not automatic. Minimum time is required for practice; with mental practice it should be available for use.

204

REAR ARM LOCK

The rear arm lock can be used as an ending technique after stopping an attack with appropriate hand or foot blows, or it can be used to regain control if an attempted arm bar is not successful.

205.   A back-handed blow is stopped with forearm blocks.

206.   You apply arm bar, which he resists by pulling his arm back.

207.   Using the energy of his effort, push him forward with your left hand as you pull his captured wrist up his back.

208.   The completed hold will allow full control for a moment. To maintain control, you can walk him forward, or put him on the ground with back takedown.

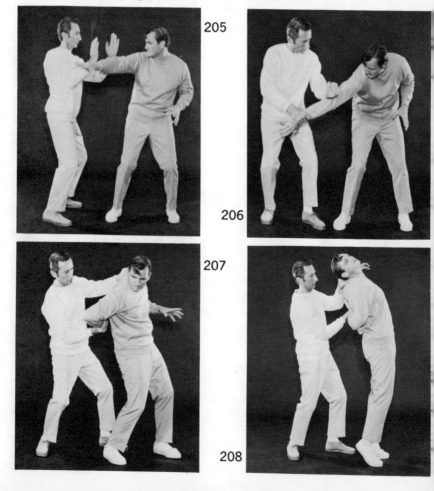

205

206

207

208

KICK-BACK TAKEDOWN

This way of putting an adversary on the ground closely resembles an actual judo throw. For self-defense you use the takedown only as an ending technique, not as your primary defense.

Practice Procedure

To learn the correct mechanics of the kick-back takedown, you will practice it in the following manner:

209.   Partners stand facing and grip each other at the upper arms (sleeves) with both hands, as shown.

210.   Take a step with your left foot to place it outside of your partner's right foot; as you step, use your arms to swivel him around and back, off-balance.

209   210

211

212

213

214

211.　Raise your right leg, fully extended, continuing the twisting action of your arms to keep your partner off-balance.

212, 213.　Swing your leg back sharply, kicking calf-to-calf; as you kick, swivel him around and down, using your arms and body action to effect the takedown.

All the actions of the takedown must be coordinated. New students commonly neglect one or the other of the two essential actions; you must twist him off-balance and you must use a swinging kick.

214.　Avoid the two mistakes shown here: The opponent has not been twisted off-balance; a push is being used, instead of a swinging kick.

SWINGING CLUB ATTACK—Block, Kick, Takedown

215.   The adversary reveals the style of the attack by his gesture.

216.   As he swings, step inside of the swinging arm and block is with double forearms (or two-handed slash).

217.   Do not attempt to take the weapon away! As you kick, clamp his arm under your arm, preventing the use of the arm or weapon.

218.   As an ending technique, you may use the leg and body takedown, or hand and foot blows until he is subdued.

215

216

217

218

GANG ATTACK

Defending against more than one opponent does not take greater skill, but it does require more determination and an understanding of the gang member. The men who need the support of a gang (a gang can be two people) to attack a victim are not brave, nor are they looking for a fight; they are looking for a victim.

A gang can rarely, if ever, be dissuaded by appeal to sympathy, though you might possibly avoid physical confrontation by a show of determination to defend yourself. Cowering before a gang will insure your being attacked. There is no guarantee that you could win against a gang, but if you don't make a spirited try, what is the alternative? Because gang members don't want to get hurt, they just want to hurt someone, the essential defense is to try to hurt one member as quickly and as much as you can. This has been a successful procedure; students report that after hurting the first member of the gang, the other or others have backed down.

One Holding, One Threatening

219.   In this first example, talk is out of the question. The attack has begun. The man holding you is not hurting you; concentrate your attack on the man in front.

220.   Kick as hard as you can, several times, if necessary, at the front man. Aim at the knee to immobilize him.

221.   When you have hurt the front man, kick at the man holding you.

222.   When you have hurt and weakened him with vigorous kicks, use a vigorous elbow blow into the body.

223.   Get around behind him and thrust him into the first man.

None of the actions for this defense are complicated or difficult; the success of such a defense would depend on your ability to control your fear enough to enter into a quick, vigorous and spirited defense, ongoing and without hesitation.

219

220

221

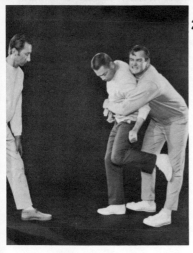

222

223

TRIPLE ACTION—Practice Procedure

The purpose of this practice is to develop your ability to respond with more than one blow at a time. Even an eager street fighter has trouble defending against two simultaneous blows; defense against three simultaneous blows is even more difficult.

Begin your practice of this procedure in slow motion. Your purpose is to learn how to deliver three blows at one time and you should practice a variety of possible triple blows. When you have learned how to make triple action defenses, increase the speed of your delivery.

Start from a relaxed position facing your partner, to simulate a non-hostile, ready stance.

224

225

224.   As he steps forward to cue the attack, kick and deliver two hand blows.

225.   Without hesitation, deliver another triple action, using different target areas.

Practice to improve your ability to use any of the hand and foot blows you have learned. Kick and hit at all the appropriate, available target areas.

When you can perform the triple action moderately well, combine it with continuing actions, for example, spin and kick into the back of the knee.

OVERHEAD CLUB ATTACK—Crossed-Arm Block and Arm Bar

226.   The type of attack is clearly indicated by the gesture.

227.   Take a deep step in and block his attacking arm at the wrist. (This block has not been shown before.) Cross your wrists and thrust sharply upward to catch his wrist.

228.   Do not attempt to take his weapon. Grip his arm.

229.   Apply arm bar.

226

227

228

229

230.   To make him release his club or stick, you can smash down onto the back of his elbow with your forearm.

230   231

REAR HEADLOCK ESCAPE

231.   Rear headlock is effected. Grip his forearm with both your hands and jerk down. This action is not likely to break his hold, but it will relieve pressure and pain.

232.   Continuing to jerk down on his arm, kick sharply into his shin, stamp on the instep and continue kicking until you feel his grip weakened.

233.   When his grip is weakened, step back, pull free.

234.   Finish with takedown, or continue hand and foot blows, as necessary.

ARM PIN ESCAPE

235.   Trying to struggle forward against the grip of a stronger person is not effective.

236.   Kick sharply into the knee or shin, several times, until you feel his grip weaken.

237.   When his grip is weakened, turn your body and pull one arm free. Continue kicking, if necessary, to complete the escape.

232

233

234

235

236

237

238.   Continue with hand and foot blows, as necessary.

238   239

FRONT BENT-ARM LOCK

239.   You apply arm bar.

240.   Your opponent resists by pulling his arm inward.

241.   Taking advantage of his action push his arm inward and upward with your right hand, allowing his captured wrist to swivel in your grip.

240   241

242.   243.

242.   Your left hand slides over his elbow and under his wrist to grip your own right wrist.

243.   Pressure is applied by taking a step forward with your right foot and placing your elbow at his face (or under his chin or at his chest). If necessary, you can walk him backward or take him to the ground.

DISTRACTION

Distraction is an excellent aid to defense. If your would-be assailant can be distracted for just a fraction of a moment, you could gain a valuable instant in which to begin your defense.

The purpose of the distraction is to make him look at or react to unexpected movement or sound. Distraction can be as subtle as a small hand movement or shifting of your eyes, or it can be a quick, lively, startling action. There are some situations in which it is not prudent to startle your adversary, for these you would use subtle distraction. There are some situations in which it is much to your advantage to startle him as much as possible.

Types of Distraction

244.   A sudden hand movement. For subtle distraction, the movement could be slight. For startling distraction, a wide gesture and a loud yell are effective.

245.   A sudden thrusting movement into his face, accompanied by a shout. The normal reaction to this kind of action is drawing the head back.

246.   Simultaneous hand and foot thrusting movements, with a loud yell.

Any object thrown into the face is distraction. Even a handkerchief, if thrown from close range can distract effectively.

244

245

246

THREE ARM LOCKS—Recovery & Counter

The traditional approach to teaching jiu jitsu or aikido holds and locks does not allow for error. It is always assumed that the student has practiced for many years and that any technique he attempts will be successful. In real life, for people with moderate skill, it is more realistic to prepare for possible mistakes or possible resistance which would invalidate the attempted technique. For this reason, you have learned ongoing defenses, even though it is likely that the first one or two actions would stop the attack. It will give you more confidence and insure your chances of being successful with your first action, if you know how to recover and counter in case first actions need follow-up.

The following procedure is practice in recovering from your errors in (or his resistance to) application on the basic arm bar.

In earlier lessons, you have learned all this material. You will now practice a smooth and correct transition from one hold to the other.

247. You apply arm lock, perhaps placing your bar too high.

248. This allows him to bend his arm upward.

247 248

249

250

251

249. You respond by attempting to apply the front bent-arm lock. He resists by straightening his arm.

250, 251. You apply rear bent-arm lock.

In street defense, the lock would be used as the ending technique and your adversary would be weakened with kicks and hand blows. This practice procedure is to develop your ability to move from one type of lock to another with correct response to his resistance—not fighting it, but taking advantage of it.

GANG ATTACK—Front Threat

When threatened by more than one assailant directly in front, it is best, if you can, to get off to one side of the group. From this position you are less vulnerable to the taack of the others as you go into action against the end man. If you cannot move out of position, and both (or all) assailants seem equally threatening, make your first move against the biggest man, or the one who appears to be spokesman or leader. This is your best chance of avoiding physical encounter with the other man. If you start your defense against the weaker or smaller man, you are vulnerable to attack from the larger assailant. Psychologically, it is disconcerting to the gang to have their biggest man taken on first. You have to defend with spirit and determination or resign yourself to the role of passive victim.

252.   Two assailants move in.

253.   Leap, step or duck to the outside of the two, and immediately kick with vigor. Try to keep this man between you and the other man as you continue kicking and hitting.

252   253

254

255

254.   Shove the first man into the second.

255.   Keep moving around, getting to the rear of the second man. Hit and kick and shove.

DEFENSE AGAINST SLASHING KNIFE OR CHAIN

Unlike a stick, a chain can whip around to hit you if you try to move in close; a slashing knife creates a wider danger area than does a stab thrust.

To evade the attack, you must leap back out of range of the chain or knife; to begin the defense actions, you will have to leap in after the attacking arm has gone by you.

256.   If attack is threatened with a chain, a wide-slashing knife, or in an ambiguous way which makes it difficult to decide the style of attack, leap back out of range of the weapon.

256

257

258

257.   Immediately take another leap to the outside of the attacking arm.

258.   Kick with force, as you grip his arm and stiffen your arms to keep him out of hitting range. Kick as necessary. Do not try to take his weapon away from him until he is completely subdued.

You and your partner can practice this fairly realistically, but do not use a real chain or knife. A blunt stick can be used to simulate the knife and a piece of rope can simulate the chain. Observe the rules of safety, a rope or stick can hurt if vigorous contact is made.

DEFENSE FROM GROUND

Taking a T-stance will help keep you from getting pushed down or losing your balance. If you do fall down and are within kicking distance of an assailant, don't try to get up —defend from the ground. If you try to rise with your head within his hand or foot range, you are vulnerable.

The purpose of this practice procedure is to learn how to swivel your body around for mobility as you kick from the supine position. If you were prone (lying face down), you would roll over, even if it involves risk of getting hurt as you roll. From a prone position you can do very little to protect yourself except hold your hands over your head and you are not able to take action against your assailant.

259   260

Practice Procedure

259.   Your partner stands just outside of kicking range.
You balance yourself on your forearms and swivel on
your buttocks so that you can move as he moves. Kick
vigorously at his shins. Keep your kicks low and snappy.

260.   As your partner runs around to try to get to your
head, swivel so that your feet are toward him, continuing to kick with force. You "lose" is he gets around to
where he could kick you in the head.

CLOSE-IN KNIFE ATTACK

DO NOT ATTEMPT A DEFENSE against a knife man
if he is using the knife as intimidation. If robbery is the
intention, and you do not feel that you will be hurt if you
are cooperative, it is foolish to attempt to counter him.
Knife defense, close-in, involves risk of being cut. You
make a defense when the only alternative is passive sub-
mission to being knifed. You make a defense which mini-
mizes the possibility of being cut critically. The traditional aikido or jiu jitsu defense against knife attack is
useless except for a person of exceptional skill. Grappling with the knife hand or trying to take the knife away
is neither prudent nor practical.

261. You are threatened by knife attack. Your judgment is that he really means to use the knife, regardless of what you do!

262. Use a very slight, subtle, hand gesture to distract him as you thrust his knife arm cross-body.

263. Grip his wrist and stiffen your arm to keep the point of the knife away from your body as you stab with your fingers into his eyes (this is an instance where eye jabs are necessary and justified).

264. Grip his arm with both hands and kick with vigor. Do not attempt to take the knife away until he is hurt and subdued.

261

262

263

264

GANG ATTACK—Cornered

If you apprise the situation as one in which both assailants are equally threatening and there is no way for you
to take action against one without being vulnerable to the
other, you should make simultaneous hand and foot
blows to both. Fast, snappy, determined, spirited defense
is your only alternative to passive acceptance of a beating.

265.   Two assailants threaten attack; there is no way of
getting out from between them.

266.   Hit one and kick the other, simultaneously.

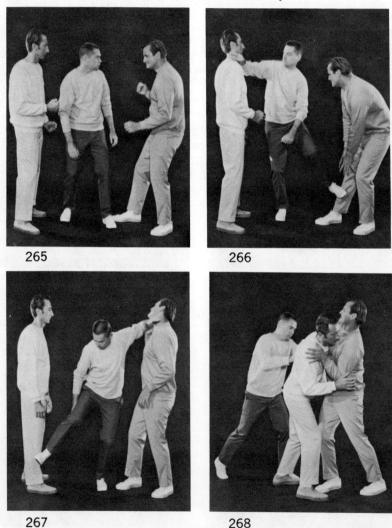

265

266

267

268

267. Without hesitation, reverse the blows and kick the one you hit and hit the one you kicked, with force and vigor!

268. Shove the weakened adversary against the other one and continue to kick and hit, as necessary.

DEFENSE FROM CAR

Prevention is the best defense. Mental preparation to take simple precautions will minimize the possibility of being threatened in your car. If you are in a situation of potential danger, roll up the windows and lock the doors, or, if you feel that you cannot avoid defending yourself, get out of the car, if possible.

269. If you cannot roll up the windows and lock the doors, open the door as he approaches and push it into him as he gets close.

270. If you cannot then close the door and drive away, get out and continue with kicks and hand blows, as necessary.

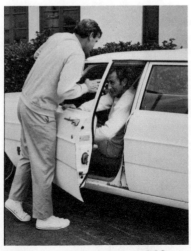

269

270

271.

271. If he approaches the car too quickly for you to open the door or roll up the window, a heel-of-palm blow into his face, or up under his chin would be effective. What you do next would depend on the particular situation. If you can drive away, of course you should. If you cannot drive away or roll up the windows, continue hand blows, or get out and carry on the defense as necessary.

DEFENSE AGAINST GUN

The most prudent protection against the possibility of gun attack is to avoid people who have guns. This might sound like a smart-aleck comment on a serious subject, but it is meant in earnest. Most gun murders are motivated. A high proportion of gun murders are committed not by "criminals" but by enraged husbands, fathers, ex-lovers, ex-friends, ex-partners and so on. If you suspect that someone who carries a grudge also carries a gun, take precautions.

There are, of course, incidents of gun murder in which the victim could neither avoid the killer nor defend himself—but in many instances the victim and the murderer were known to each other and prevention was at least a possibility if caution had been exercised.

When a gun is used as intimidation, as in the case of armed robbery, the robber prefers not to use his gun, especially if he is a professional. Quiet cooperation is the most prudent behavior if you are confronted by an armed

robber! Gun defense is risky; to risk death or serious injury in defense of possessions is a poor gamble. Make
mental preparation to respond appropriately if threatened by an armed assailant. Don't act out of panic or
rage.

Gun defenses are not easy; they require constant practice.
Individuals who are in professions which require vigi-
lance against gun attack need thorough training, high
skill, and the ability to defend against a variety of types of
gun attacks. For the layman, for the person of moderate
skill, this is not possible. The gun threat which you might
possibly defend against is only one of many and it is not
the most common. You can practice this defense with
your partner (using a toy gun for simulating the attack)
but you should be fully aware of the danger of attempting
defense against a gun. You should think of this as an
emergency procedure which has very little likelihood of
being used.

272.   Gun is held close. This is not a common gun
threat. If the primary motive is robbery—QUIET CO-
OPERATION is the prudent procedure!

273.   If you are convinced that he means to use the
gun and that there is no alternative to making the defense
attempt, start the defense with a very subtle distraction,
such as wiggling your fingers. A wide gesture or a scream
could make him shoot; you are not trying to startle him.

272   273

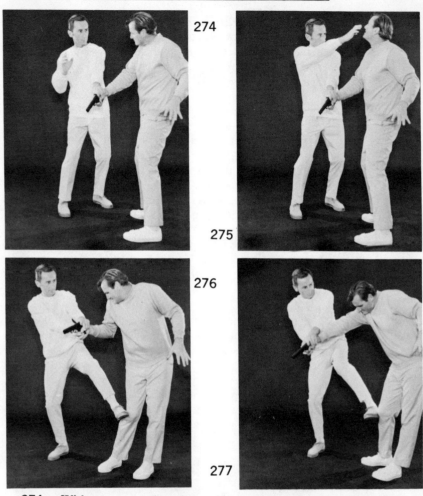

274

275

276

277

274.   With a snappy thrusting movement, hit his gun hand cross-body away from you. Your hand clasps his hand, preventing the firing of the gun. You are not trying to take the weapon away, you are deflecting the muzzle (in case the gun goes off) and you are trying to stop the action of the gun.

275.   Keeping your arm stiffened to hold his hand out of your body range, use finger stabs into the eyes (justified and necessary in this instance).

276.   Forceful kicks into the knee and shin, as you clasp both hands onto the gun hand to prevent firing.

277.   Pull his arm completely past your body for greatest safety. Clasp his arm with both your hands and continue kicking until he is hurt and subdued. Do not attempt to take his gun away until he is hurt or on the ground!

For basic, practical self-defense, it is important to know a small group of effective techniques which you can remember easily.

If, after finishing the ten lessons in this course, you do not feel confident of your ability to use the material, it is best to repeat the course. Do not attempt to learn additional techniques unless you feel thoroughly comfortable with the basic techniques. If you have any problems with the basic material, it would only intensify your problems to attempt additional techniques or more complicated material.

For functional self-defense you do not need championship skill, so you do not have to engage in rigorous training or conditioning. After you become moderately adept at the basic techniques, an occasional run-through of the defense and some occasional mental practice should keep your proficiency at the functional level.

Mental practice does not mean that you brood or worry about the possibility of assault; it means mental review of possible responses to common types of assault. When you have prepared yourself to cope with the emergency of assault, you do not have to worry about it as much as when you felt inadequate to deal with the situation.

FURTHER STUDY

If you wish to develop more than functional skill in self-defense or if you wish to continue practice as a physical fitness program, or if you have become interested in a specific specialty of weaponless fighting, you can do further work at home, you might wish to join a class, or you might be interested in organizing a group to practice with.

Most of the people who are interested in self-defense and related fighting skills do not have access to personal instruction. Only those individuals who live in some big cities have any choice of schools or teachers. Hopefully, "Y"s and civic recreation centers will offer classes in judo, karate and aikido for sport and physical fitness. Hopefully, physical education departments will expand their programs of basic self-defense offered in secondary schools. This would be the best solution to the problem of lack of training centers for the many young people interested in the subject field.

SELF-DEFENSE, JUDO, KARATE, AIKIDO: The Differences

For physical fitness or recreation it does not matter at all whether you practice sport forms of judo or karate, traditional forms of aikido or jiu jitsu, or a modern style of self-defense.

Though there are dozens and dozens of names for the various forms of Oriental fighting skills, they all fall roughly into four main groups. If you do plan to enroll in a school and you have choices, the brief descriptions which follow may guide you to the specialty you prefer.

Sport judo involves mainly falling and throwing techniques. If you observe new students practicing falls only and if throws are being practiced as the principal technique, you are observing a sport judo class. The throws of judo are taught as though they were useful for self-defense, but in my opinion judo is marvellous for people who enjoy body-contact contest and want vigorous physical activity.

Contest karate involves development of a very high level of technical skill in the performance of hand and foot blows. The method of practice is generally divided into four parts. 1. A good deal of time is spent doing calisthenics. 2. The new student practices single hand or foot blows or stances over and over and over until he has perfected each single technique. 3. He practices the "forms" of karate in solo or two-man routines. Every step is rehearsed and practiced in a formal pre-arranged sequence. 4. He practices contest-like sparring in which there are rigid rules limiting the target areas for points and limiting the types of blows which are permitted in contest. Contest karate is excellent for those who enjoy working toward perfection of technique and for those who enjoy training for tournament.

Aikido is a highly stylized specialty of weaponless fighting in which pressures and twists are applied against the joints. The techniques themselves are related to holds and locks, but the manner of practicing them involves rolling out of the holds so that it appears that the person practicing the techniques has thrown his opponent. There is a current fad for aikido as self-defense which is totally unrelated to its practical uses.

Aikido is fun to practice and it has great benefits as a fitness activity, but because it takes so long to learn and because fantastically high skill is required for its application in an assault situation, only the exceptional person could possibly expect to use it as self-defense.

Jiu jitsu is a catch-all term which is used for a number of old-style self-defense methods. Jiu jitsus share the characteristic of combining groups of techniques. Some combine throws with hand and foot blows; some use holds and locks in combination with throwing techniques; some use throws and control holds. There are styles of jiu jitsu which use all three groups of techniques. Jiu jitsu does not involve contest or contest-like practice procedures.

Although my method of self-defense derives from the principles of jiu jitsu, there are two major differences. Old-style jiu jitsu training still includes defenses against kneeling sword attack and similar situations which the modern student is unlikely to encounter. Modern self-defense should be concerned with more relevant kinds of possible assault. Old-style jiu jitsus practice defenses as a specific response to a specific attack. Far less time is involved in learning a small group of techniques which can be used in a variety of attack situations. Far less time is involved in learning practical, adequate material for functional street defense than is spent in rehearsing the great number of "tricks" of jiu jitsu.

CHOOSING A SCHOOL

If you live in a community which has a school, visit it, observe a class in session and then you can decide whether or not the teacher suits you. If there is more than one school, visit them and compare. You are the best judge of what is best for you even though you do not have any technical background. You are equipped with a more important gauge for making a decision— your own reaction to what you see!

Any reliable school or teacher will allow you to observe at least one complete session before you make up your mind. Verbal explanations of what is being taught are not enough; you have to see what it is. Nor should you allow yourself to be dazzled by what the teacher himself can do. You are not paying to see him perform; you are paying him for what he can teach *you* to do.

When you observe a class, watch the teacher and watch the students. Does the teacher actually instruct? Does he give clear directions and explain what is to be done, or does he merely demonstrate and leave the students to imitate as well as they can? Is the teacher patient and does he encourage the students, or is he cross and rude to students who need correction or help?

Do the students seem enthusiastic about what they are doing? Do they appear to be helpful to one another? Is there a friendly atmosphere?

Is the material being practiced what you think *you* would like to learn?

If you like what you see, the school is right for you. If you don't like what you see, the school is not right for you, even though the teacher, the material and the method might be quite acceptable to other individuals.

DON'T SIGN A CONTRACT unless you are absolutely certain that you understand what you are signing and that it is a fair contract. Unless you are familiar with contracts, you may need help in deciding whether or not the contract protects your consumer rights. If you sign a contract without reading or understanding it, you may find yourself obligated to pay for lessons you don't want to take or you may find that you cannot get a refund in case of emergency.

As a general rule, you are better protected if you make partial payments as you go along than if you pay for a full course in advance. If you make partial payments, then, if you change your mind or lose interest, or move, you are not tied to an arrangement which might be a financial burden.

If you need help in deciding if a contract is fair, if a financial arrangement is fair, or if the operator of a school is reliable, ask your local Chamber of Commerce or your librarian to direct you. Most communities have agencies which offer free advice and guidance in these matters.

It is your money and your time which are being spent. You have the right to spend them the way you please and to make sure that you will get your money's worth.

WHO CAN TEACH

It is a common misconception that only a black belt holder can teach self-defense and related fighting skills. It is a mistake to think that the requirements for earning a black belt degree include preparation or skill to teach.

A black belt indicates a high degree of achievement. Much time and effort go into that achievement. But it does not necessarily follow that a black belt holder is a competent teacher. Most black belts are awarded for excellence in contest—winning in tournament. The qualities which make a tournament champion are not those which make an outstanding teacher. In every type of activity which requires physical training you will find examples of good teachers who are not necessarily good performers and you will find excellent performers who are not skilled teachers. This field is no different. Physical education teachers are proving this point dramatically. Throughout the United States, many physical education teachers, men and women, are teaching successful classes of basic self-defense in secondary schools. Although they have not had previous experience in this specialty and though they do not have belt degrees, they are particularly well-suited to the instruction of basic self-defense because they are teachers. Physical directors of recreation centers are also teaching basic self-defense with good results. Such teachers understand community needs, they are sensitive to the fact that defenses must be modern, safe and socially acceptable; they do not confuse the modern urban community with the setttings of Samurai warrior movies.

INDEX

**BRUCE TEGNER BOOKS ARE SOLD IN BOOKSTORES
THROUGHOUT THE WORLD**

If your book or magazine dealer does not have the other titles you want, he can order them for you, or you can order direct from the publisher.

For description of all the books by Bruce Tegner, and order form, write to:

THOR BOOKS
Box 1782
Ventura, Calif. 93001